VISION
POWERED
MANAGEMENT

BOB COLLINS
with ROBERT STILLMAN

VISION
POWERED
MANAGEMENT

...a leadership process for shaping 21st century management

outskirts
press

Dedication

To my family, especially my wife, Andrea, for their encouragement and patience during the writing period. To Robert Stilllman, for his suggestion to finish writing Vision Powered Management, including his editing and writing contributions. To my daughter Leslie, for her devotion and skills in formatting and editing the manuscript. To Bill Shenkir, for his suggestions on content and headlining methods, and finally, to Brian Murphy, for his thoughtful comments.

Table of Contents

Foreword

This is an idea born from two entirely different brains. I first met Robert Collins by chance (and to my mind there was some destiny behind it as well) in a restaurant in Marco Island, Florida. One of the things that came from that first chance meeting is this book.

In our initial introductions to each other, I learned he was an accomplished business leader, having retired from General Electric (GE) in 1998. I told him about my work in teaching and coaching business leaders of all stripes through the Center for Leadership Development at New Horizons.

During our discussion, I shared my frustration with the methods and models that are being taught to tomorrow's leaders as not being as clear as I would like. I spoke about the theories being explained and understood but not enough about the "how to do it" category. This initial meeting led to another meeting where we discussed the state of leadership development today.

Both of us seemed to orbit around the important need for leaders to lead with vision. Since the business books section is awash with different takes on what it means to be a visionary leader, a bit of history as to how we are approaching this subject might be in order.

In 2003, Richard Boyatzis, Annie McKee, and Daniel Goleman teamed up to publish *Primal Leadership, Realizing the Power of Emotional Intelligence*.[1] In the book, the authors point to research that indicates successful leaders consistently shift between one of six leadership styles.

They argue that of the six, there are two "dissonant" styles (or styles that can be useful for short periods of time but, if overused, can harm the morale of the organization) and four "resonant" styles, which build positive morale in the long term. One of the resonant styles, and the one they suggest is the most effective, is the style they coined: Visionary Leader.

In brief, the visionary leadership style is appropriate when an organization is stuck and in need of a fire lit under the employees. This style is successful in reigniting passion and commitment to the work at hand and is a "go-to" style when a turnaround is needed.

In my study of leadership, going back to my earliest days in the business world, I have studied and now teach from the likes of Robert K. Greenleaf's "Servant Leadership" to today's iterations of Kouzes and Posner's "Transformational Leadership" model, among others.

It was Goleman, as well as others in the emotional intelligence camp, who took the empirical data that proved that EQ

---

1   (Boyatzis, McKee, & Goleman, 2002)

(emotional quotient) was a key element in leading high-performing teams. Their work with organizations like Johnson & Johnson and others made an impact on the business world. It was largely due to this empirical evidence that I chose to pursue certification in EQ as a practitioner and an assessor after my master's work.

The difficulty, of course, with any behavioral skill training is that it takes patience and can be easily thrown away after consuming. Advances in the study of the human brain give us insight into the learning of hard skills and so-called soft skills. In the 2013 updated edition of *Primal Leadership*, the difference in learning hard versus soft skills is laid out:

"Skills based in the limbic areas [EQ skills such as self-awareness, self-management, recognizing patterns, and empathy, to name a few] *research shows, are best learned through motivation, extended practice and feedback. Compare that kind of learning with what goes on in the neocortex, which governs analytical and technical ability. The neocortex grasps concepts quickly placing them within an expanding network of associations and comprehension. This part of the brain for instance can figure out from reading a book how to use a computer program, or the basics of making a sales call. When learning technical or analytical skills, the neocortex operates with magnificent efficiency."* [2]

I didn't know it at the time, but as I sat with Bob Collins in his home office in beautiful Marco Island, we had an interesting combination of skills. Bob is Mr. Neocortex; I'm Mr. Limbic. I just had a hunch that there was some combination of our experiences that could help fill the "what it is" versus "how to do" void. And

2   (Goleman, Boyatzis, & McKee, 2013) pg. 102

then Bob revealed something that shot my interest level through the roof.

"I had started a book," he said. The book he started was not only meant to reflect on what he had learned about leading and managing with vision—it was a method based on an actual practice that he had used repeatedly in his successful career.

Bob's accomplishments are well documented. He is known for taking over Jack Welch's industrial automation project at GE. He also has done quite a bit of consultative work post-GE, in retirement. Here was someone who had taken several companies, ranging in size from $100 million to $1.8 billion a year, and turned them around using the model he will share in this book. My own vision started taking shape.

"You dipped your peanut butter in my chocolate." The old Reese's Peanut Butter Cup ad from long ago came to my mind as Bob started sharing his accomplishments. At some point in the conversation, one of us suggested, "What if we could put a playbook-style manual together that any newly anointed leader, or even one who has taken over a new team, could pick up to start implementing a visionary style to lead their teams to success?"

Could such a playbook be written by the Jack Welch disciple steeped in no excuses and pragmatic and measured performance (Mr. Neocortex) if…he was teamed up with a learning and development professional (Mr. Limbic) who pushed every chapter to reveal the pragmatic "What do I put on my calendar first thing Monday morning?" style of learn/apply/reflect?

The first line of this forward stated, "This is an idea born from two entirely different brains." This book looks to glean the wisdom of a proven business leader through the filter of an application bias. We as the authors would like to express that our genuine hope is for you to come away with actionable items to apply to your workplace leadership challenges.

If when picking up this book, you knew the question rattling in your head was "How do I practice being a visionary leader?" then the answer comes to us in Bob Collins's telling of his story throughout this book. He writes in the first person, and we hope that your observance of his account can give you the wisdom of a veteran of the turnaround game. As these techniques and examples guide you, we would love to hear from you on the progress of your journey. Enjoy.

Robert D. Stillman, MATD

CHAPTER 1:

Introduction

J ack Welch and I joined GE the same year, in 1960, in the same town, Pittsfield, Massachusetts. It was my first assignment after graduating from Manhattan College with an honors degree in electrical engineering. Pittsfield was a midsize city, and GE was its largest employee by far. GE's businesses there encompassed a large industrial division and an aerospace division.

Pittsfield was a blue-collar town surrounded by arts and festival activities, mostly centered in the nearby small town of Lenox. Arthur Fiedler and the Boston Pops concerts and Jacobs Pillow, the internationally acclaimed dance center, were the highlights of the summer and fall seasons there. Pittsfield also had its own small ski facility on Bosquet Mountain, which helped to make the wintertime pass by faster.

This aerospace GE division designed and manufactured a guidance system that directs the pathway of a missile launched from an underwater submarine location to a designated site. The GE division was located on a large campus and housed several thousand employees. It was a secure, gated facility, and personnel had to have classified clearances to work there.

In 1960, the U.S. Navy began to deploy nuclear-powered submarines armed with 16 Polaris missiles each. Each missile was 31 feet long and 4.5 feet in diameter and was powered by two solid-fueled stages. Three models were developed, one with a range of 1,400 miles and a one-megaton nuclear warhead; another with a 1,700-mile range and a one-megaton warhead; and finally, one capable of delivering three 200-kiloton warheads 2,800 miles. The missiles would be fired while the sub was under the water, largely undetected by unfriendly nations such as Russia.

The program was a high-priority program where the Navy officials overseeing the program wore special uniforms, worked five-and-a-half day weeks, had mail forwarded "High Priority" (no email at that time), and used the slogan "think big and fast or get out." This rubbed off on me and the work atmosphere at the GE division.

It was at this early stage in my career when, in addition to my day job, I experienced my first transformational training through GE's manufacturing management program that required after-work tailored education classes in a variety of subjects.

One of the most beneficial night courses this program offered was a six-week course in public speaking. This course required me to select a subject, write the speech, and then deliver the speech to the group of my fellow students. They would in turn critique it and offer constructive ideas of how to improve the content and one's oral delivery style.

Prior to this, I was an engineering nerd and had never done any real public speaking and as a result, I had much to learn. I had little self-confidence in doing it and much to practice. At the end of the course, each student had to present a speech on any topic of their choosing and do it in competition with the other students. I came in second out of 19 in the competition. I had been transformed from a nervous, low-confident public speaker to someone with a learned technique and newly gained self-confidence, while enjoying the process of doing so.

I found later that it was one of the most indispensable skills needed in implementing the Vision-Powered Management (VPM) process.

Many stories about employees who worked in a smaller, undistinguished building on campus, whose lights remained on well into the night, were rampant then. The stories spoke to the long hours worked, the loud and boisterous afterwork parties held there, and the very energetic guy heading up that business. I was told that it housed the seedling start-up Lexan plastic business.

Lexan plastic was a new "wonder discovery" from the famous GE Laboratory near Schenectady that could revolutionize the plastics industry. Not too many years later, it developed into a multibillion-dollar GE business. As it turns out Jack Welch was the person leading that business, and it was where he etched his initial reputation in the company.

After Pittsfield, I had assignments in the GE consumer products, power generation, and industrial divisions. Upon graduation from the management program, I took on permanent assignments in the aircraft equipment division.

On December 28, 1968, Apollo 8, manned by Jim Lovell, Frank Borman, and the flight engineer Bill Anders, splashed down in the Atlantic Ocean after successfully completing the first ever mission to circle the moon and back. Apollo 8 was another step in the grand vision of President John F. Kennedy, who just six years and three months earlier gave his speech to 40,000 people in the Rice University Stadium, building the case for going to the moon. He compared the mission to being like other "hard" things, like climbing a mountain, or Rice playing Texas. His words were "We choose to go to the moon in this decade and do the other things, not because they are easy, but because they are hard, because that goal will serve to organize and measure the best of our energies and skills, because that challenge is one that we are willing to accept, one we are unwilling to postpone, and one which we intend to win, and the others, too."

As things turned out, Bill Anders, the aforementioned flight engineer on that Apollo mission, found his way to GE as the newly appointed VP of its aircraft equipment division unit. It just so happens I was the newly appointed general manager of a troubled business now reporting to Bill.

Bill was a great mentor and taught me a lot. I learned not just from his style, but I studied and emulated in my own way his unique thought process. Bill first always wanted to focus on the facts of a situation, what alternative solutions were considered, what were the expected outcomes, and what were the major considerations influencing the recommended decision. He also wove into his business review questions that addressed the degree of risk in embarking on certain business opportunities. His training as an astronaut, where risk assessment was crucial, most likely became part of his management DNA. I utilized that lesson extensively in my career. With the increasing technology complexities of 21st-century business activities, risk management is a skill that current and tomorrow's leaders must learn and utilize. I especially appreciated his positive way of second-guessing and his ability to add value to the final decision process.

As part of his mentoring, Bill asked me to present to Jack Welch and his staff at an upcoming business review meeting. Jack's team members would include some of his direct reports like the VP of finance, VP of human relations, corporate counsel, VP of international business, etc. These business reviews were a regular part of the GE culture and their business process. The reviews encompassed discussion of current and forecasted financial results versus budget, the outlook for the next year, and actions being taken to further improve business performance. Many times, it would include meeting upcoming high-potential individuals fondly referred to as "Hipots," short for "high potentials."

It was at that business review where I presented the results from the actions that my business team had implemented to significantly improve the health of this business. Such actions included expanded marketing efforts to increase sales volume, improving profit margins through vigorous cost reduction programs, stronger emphasis on free cash flow through inventory and receivables reductions, and more active employee involvement in quality improvement. Jack invited me that night to sit next to him at dinner. This was shortly after he had succeeded Reg Jones as CEO and chairman of GE, who had served in that position from 1972 to 1981. During dinner, Jack asked me a lot of questions about my background, education, career in GE to date, including what I had accomplished in previous GE business assignments.

Little did I realize that this was one of Jack's ways of discovering people who could be called on to solve problems in other businesses needing such help. Shortly thereafter, I was fortunate to be selected to take on additional high-level assignments. Bill Anders, ever the flight engineer, along with Jack Welch's mentoring, "launched" my career to higher levels in GE.

Fast-forward from start to finish, a total of 38 years was dedicated to applying my craft at GE. There were many professional development opportunities through those years, including having access to the GE management school of hard knocks and being a frequent participant in GE's in-house training programs at the world-class GE Management Development Institute located in Crotonville, New York. The business management and executive development courses were especially helpful and were taught by some of the best graduate school professors, such as Ram Sharam.

The exposure to world-class university scholars at GE Crotonville, coupled with the lessons learned from legendary GE leaders, such as Reg Jones, Jack Welch, Gerhard Neuman, Bill Anders, and Larry Bossidy, broadened, sharpened, and matured my skills significantly. As a result, most of my assignments occurred in underperforming technology businesses that needed reshaping and improved performance. Over those years, I gained a reputation of being a fixer, since during those assignments, my business teams faced and resolved a variety of issues that had contributed to underperformance. At the same time, I was formalizing many of the processes that are discussed in this book.

Just prior to retirement from GE, I started to write a book describing the management processes I utilized that provided the road maps my teams used in improving those businesses. I had created a title for the book of *Vision Powered Management, VPM* for short, and had written a few chapters of the book. What I did not anticipate was how busy I would become in the consulting and land development businesses I created immediately upon retirement. The book I had hoped to complete early in my retirement (the one you are reading now) sat unfinished on my bookshelf for 16 years!

My post-GE career included becoming chairman of the board of two public companies along with director positions in start-up businesses. Each of those assignments allowed me to pass on to those companies the helpful ideas and methods that are discussed in *Vision-Powered Management*. In every case except one, improved results occurred. During the diagnosis process part of VPM, in the one exception I just mentioned, it was discovered that inappropriate methods had been used in reporting sales to distributors. This required that previous financial reporting had to be restated, and the losses were significantly worse. Furthermore, the product lines had not kept up technologically, and the business competitiveness was suffering significantly. Conditions were such that the business could not continue and had to be shut down.

In another case, a business had stitched together a $1.8 billion collection of businesses through acquisitions. There was very little synergy between any of the businesses, and overall financial results were poor. Also, many of the board of directors had very little experience in the markets and products of those businesses. The stock was selling around $11 per share on Nasdaq. Shortly after being invited to be a board member, I analyzed the historical financial performance of each of the businesses over a three-year period. The analysis included market share, sales, product margins, overhead costs, operating margin, and free cash flow. Each business was then put into a bucket based on its performance. There were three buckets, growing profitable business, mature profitable business, and underperforming business. By doing so, it served to differentiate how financial resources and strategies should be developed and applied. We created a small team of board members to develop a restructuring plan that included creating a vision for what we wanted the company to be, determining those businesses that needed to be fixed or sold, maintaining those that were stable and profitable, and nourishing the ones where sales and profit growth was likely. During that time, several board positions became open and were filled with people who had direct experience in many of the businesses. Twenty-four months later, after implementation of the plan, when the underperforming businesses were either fixed, sold, or closed, the remaining businesses were growing and profitable, and the stock had grown to $18 per share. It was evident that the VPM process worked both inside and outside GE.

Fast-forward to the end of 2018; my wife, Andrea, and I were sitting in a local restaurant on a warm Marco Island, Florida, afternoon, seated by the bar. We spend our winters and early springs there, and it's funny how Florida is perceived as a place where "just the old people live."

Now, it is true there are numerous retirees in Florida, and Marco Island is no different than other parts of Florida. I bring up this perception because a former GE protégé of mine told me he met Jack Welch there recently. Jack also winters in Florida. During his business conversation, he told Jack that Andrea and I lived in Marco. Jack responded, "Oh, Marco is where the old people in Florida live." I thought to myself, "Oh my God, he also spends wintertime in Florida, he is several years older than me, and so Marco is the only place where the old people live!?" I always get a kick out of that comment.

Getting back to the dinner Andrea and I were having at the restaurant we wound up sitting next to a couple. The male was about six foot four inches or so, with a booming voice, and his friend was a petite, attractive, friendly woman with a much quieter voice. We struck up a conversation, learning about each other. As you learned in the foreword, his name was Bob Stillman, and we both shared a common interest in management processes, leadership characteristics, and skills.

During the conversation, I spoke briefly about the book I started writing 16 years ago that was sitting on my shelf unfinished, which included a how-to management process I had used while in GE and in my consulting business. I explained that the book, which I had titled *Vision-Powered Management*, described a leadership methodology that was powered by creating a vision of the business. The vision stated the purpose of the business, including establishing goals, implementation strategies and tactics for improvement, measurements for progress along the way, and celebrations for success. Bob asked if I would consider discussing this further, and so we got together at my home office several days later for further discussion.

This is basically what I proceeded to tell Bob that day. Vision Powered Management starts with the answer first. The key lever to sustainable business success is repeatable high productivity in every aspect of the business, whether it be products, service, sales, and the like. Why? Simply put, today's global economy is value driven. No longer can you have the best product, best quality and service, and highest price.

Apple may be learning that lesson these days as the sales of their flagship cell phones start to slow, or even decay, as consumers consider lower-priced technically competitive offerings. Today you must do everything well and be a low-cost/low-price provider. How do you accomplish this? Your business must achieve the highest levels of productivity over your competition in every category of work you do, at a significant differential.

There is not a business in existence that isn't in need of some improvement. During my career, I always encountered opportunities to apply the principles of what I learned about improving results. Vision Powered Management is a process that incorporates those principles and can identify financial issues and inefficiencies of all types, prioritize areas needing improvement, and unleash any held-back personnel productivity of every organization. It operates on the basis that many organizations accomplish their business activities with as little as 30 percent of the workforce performing to their maximum skills capacities. (I have seen studies where the number is as low as 17 percent.) The other 70 percent hold back for a variety of reasons and factors. These factors could include insufficient training or lack of self-confidence in themselves or the business leadership, or they are turned off by the methods and attitudes of management, or by monotony in the job, or lack of commitment to the purpose of the business. Studies have shown that companies that have achieved a high number of employees performing to their maximum skill levels enjoy operating margins that are three times higher than those with low levels of employee engagement. High numbers of employees working at their maximum energy and skill level are based on "want to" versus "have to." High performance levels occur when peoples' attitudes transform to team goals in lieu of a personal job focus. Employees transform from being observers to players when the organization has changed from bureaucratic to dynamic and agile.

The Vision Powered Management process eliminates the negative factors, overcomes the lack of employee commitment, and can result in two to three times more people working at their fullest capacity. It is a methodology that ties its employees to the purpose, goals, and objectives of the business. It places appropriate and necessary emphasis on "human-ware" and "techno-ware." To become a high-performance organization with high employee involvement and performance levels, a company must do some basic blocking and tackling. This includes setting a clear vision of the purpose of the business, clearly identifying actions it wants to take, articulating an action plan, putting in place robust review processes to assure success, and finally, establishing accountability for all. VPM provides a road map to accomplish this.

It requires that a business define in concise terms what it wants its future to be and how it must be developed by a very large segment of its workforce. Like President Kennedy's ideas at Rice Stadium, the vision must be oriented toward the future, identify important objectives, strategies, and goals, and provide for flexibility, while at the same time providing a sense of stability.

Managers must be converted from cops to coaches, and the process turns the organization upside down. Coaches are on the sidelines setting demanding goals, calling the plays, shifting people to better-fitting jobs, and providing training and necessary resources to get the job done. Frontline personnel are focused on satisfying the customers and meeting and exceeding the established goals.

The process fosters the adoption of technology for speed and simplicity of operations, for higher productivity and quality, and instead of technology eliminating jobs, it increases employment emanating from higher levels of revenue.

Vision Powered Management is about reengineering, reeducation, and frequent communication of results versus goals. It is a process that focuses on:

- Creating purpose of the organization and business
- Specifying demanding goals and objectives
- Generating belief of the purpose of the business by the workforce
- Gaining commitment to achieve the goals
- Implementing improvements to satisfy achievement of the goals and objectives
- Unleashing the personal performance capacity of the workers and then refueling the process with employee rewards, pats on the back, and celebrations of success

The process is described in further detail in chapter 4, "Implementation." It only works with the absolute commitment of top-level management. It also requires endless hours to see it through, and it cannot be delegated. It must be driven by the top. Vision Powered Management can be your recipe to invent or re-invent your business for these challenging times. Finally, not only does it improve the business, it also enhances your own personal reputation.

Bob Stillman discussed in detail his work in this area, and we both felt we should consider some type of effort to create a nuts-and-bolts document offering our combined thought on this subject and offer it under the title *Vision Powered Management*.

Each chapter in the book will feature **takeaways** in a summarization at the end. The major **takeaways** from this discussion are as follows:

I.   Learn to be an effective, confident, and convincing speaker. There are numerous courses available that address this subject.

II.   Seek out a mentor you can learn from and one who can steer you in directions that will help you personally, as well as with problem analysis and solution suggestions.

III.   Every business needs a stated purpose, to have clearly identified goals, stated objectives that support achieving the goals, detailed strategies and tactics that identify the how-to actions necessary for achieving the goals, ways to frequently measure progress, celebrations of success, and formal methods to communicate and offer feedback on the progress along the way.

CHAPTER 2:

The Beginning

Although George H. W. Bush and I never met, I learned a lesson from his actions as president and commander in chief. Despite the overwhelming success of the Desert Storm operation in the Middle East counteracting Hussein's invasion of Kuwait, Bush's approval ratings suffered badly.

His predecessor, Ronald Reagan, had held forth a consistent clear vision of his America for all to see. His vision was as follows: "We must achieve the global elimination of nuclear weapons through verifiable treaties, while simultaneously developing a missile defense shield capable of protecting against cheaters and rogue nations. Once developed, we must then share it with the Russians in order to eliminate any instability of relationships that would be caused by a potential imbalance of our nuclear forces if only we were to have such an extensive missile defense system." Reagan's genius was that he understood that our national security was dependent on Russia's nuclear powers feeling equally secure. In other words, his vision of common security was that our own security was ultimately dependent on Russia's security. He communicated it frequently to all Americans as well as other countries. Embraced or shunned, that vision stood fast and strong in the minds of all people throughout his term, and to this day he is remembered as the Great Communicator.

Bush, however, was unable to produce a vision for his America that the population could embrace. His opponent in the upcoming election was Bill Clinton. Clinton developed his vision and promised to deliver it if elected president. His vision was as follows: "Our challenge today is to recognize that this is the time of transition and we must respond to it. I honestly believe the issue is not less government, and the issue is not more government. The issue is what kind of government we are going to have." Clinton put forth his ideas to build further on this claim throughout the election process. America watched as Bush's lack of a compelling vision propelled the Clinton campaign down Pennsylvania Avenue into the White House in 1992.

I was the VP of a newly formed GE business during that period that had been struggling. We were suffering from product and financial difficulties. I recognized that my team needed to clearly and quickly map out a new "game plan" detailing what needed to change and why.

The team needed to develop a vision for success and connect everything that needed to get done back to that vision. It would only be through a well-defined and demanding set of objectives, goals, and implementation strategies that would enable our business to move forward with a high level of confidence in our success.

The gladiatorial competitive environment that heated up in the '80s required that the business really stretch to take on highly challenging plans. In addition to the plans and goals, it was mandatory to set a completely new "atmosphere" among the employees, one that was highly charged and focused on success. It was necessary to get the commitment of most every employee to support the vision so that it became theirs and to unleash higher levels of their energies focused on achieving success.

The vision had to be backed up by creating an all-employee team environment that was highly involved in the determination of what steps needed to be taken to achieve a desired level of performance. There also had to be a new, highly charged "sense of urgency" atmosphere injected into the business directed at achieving the necessary results.

As mentioned in chapter 1, I had seen this work when President Kennedy created the vision of America being the first nation to reach the moon. He made a clear statement of technical superiority to the balance of the world. NASA was created and challenged to make that happen on an extremely short timetable to beat the Russians to the moon.

Building on the Reagan, Kennedy, and Clinton approach, coupled with my experiences with improving previous businesses, business improvement can most always be achieved by developing a vision, backed by highly challenging ideas, plans, and actions that are seen by your team as highly desirable and rewarding.

One early experience of mine involved a product that was used on a military aircraft actively employed in the Middle East war theater. On several occasions, the electrical generator suffered a small local conflagration resulting in smoke filtering into the cockpit area. The pilot then had to abort the mission.

It was necessary to visit several airbases and interview the pilots to be able to determine the details of the flight, such as the angle of attack at the time of conflagration, the engine RPMs, and the altitude. The events were serious enough that the customer was considering the replacement of our product with one from a competitor of ours unless we could quickly eliminate the problem from reoccurring.

I immediately appointed a team and charged them to come back in 24 hours with a plan and recommendations that would lead to a solution of the failure mode in five days.

The next morning, the team recommended the following plan. Because the product was mostly destroyed by the conflagration, it was necessary to reproduce the failure mode in a laboratory, simulating the same conditions as experienced in the aircraft at the time of failure. The team established an around-the-clock plan for the environmental testing, the product functions to be monitored, the schedules, etc., aimed at finding and fixing the problem.

On day two, we had replicated the problem. On day five, they had defined and verified a fix in the laboratory test. On day six, the customer was notified that we had replicated the failure mode and defined a fix. On day seven, they had developed a schedule plan to hand-carry the first fixed product for installation on an aircraft for verification of the fix.

In addition, the factory proceeded to build replacement products for the fleet. Fortunately, several weeks later, the customer reported that the revised product performed successfully, and we began to deliver new products with the fix installed.

I learned from experiences such as this that objectives, strategies, tactics, implementation plans, etc., need to be developed by those involved in the process. The results need to be perceived as challenging, worthwhile, achievable, and embraceable, and then they become powered through by those involved in the process.

When I say powered through, it means the people involved have adopted the process in mind, body and soul so that it can succeed. Out of these experiences came away a structured process—or style of managing—that I call Vision Powered Management, or VPM for short.

The bold promise of this book is the following: although some of these tools are not new, I found a management philosophy and structure to pull them together to effectively poke a new hole in the corporate sound barrier of past times. Establishing a business environment that gains the commitment and high performance of most every employee in support of demanding business results is key.

The Vision Powered Management process engages the tenets of management and of human involvement. There are four things to understand and be ready to commit to before implementing:

First, a sense of purpose on the job is as fundamental to a person's existence as the need for food, shelter, and companionship. By creating a clear, understandable vision for the business, backed by quantified and challenging plans and goals, the purpose of everybody's work becomes clear and focus on commitment and achievement takes hold. A properly developed business vision will ripple through the management system and put it on course for continuous improvement.

Second, it is necessary to quickly instill change in order that the employees realize that the business activities are going to be more urgent and different. Change includes requiring a higher pace of work, faster communications, and organization changes and eliminating unnecessary activities.

Third, significant training of the management team and the workforce is going to be necessary to both modify behavior and introduce needed skills.

Fourth, revised organization structures will be necessary and new equipment and software technology investments may be necessary.

Organization structure and culture are also important. A lot has been written about delayering, empowerment, work teams, and the like. You will see mention of these in the book, and they are a part of VPM. These tools also need realistic doses of "old-fashioned" techniques mixed in, such as requiring numbers on anything worthwhile to do, tasks being assigned and tracked, measurements of progress made, and a stubborn commitment to achieve the intended results.

"Nothing good comes easy" has always been my motto in life and business. At the same time, be ready to shed some of the security blankets that have served you in the past, such as multiple layers in management and bureaucratic approval requirements. In today's competitive environment, they will weigh you down like medieval armor. Expect to go through a revolution in your previous management beliefs.

No longer can you run your business on a monthly reporting basis; instead, go daily or weekly or sometimes hourly, depending on your business. Monthly or quarterly surprises are no longer tolerable. You must be transparent about problems, and you must swallow hard when owning up to your problems or mistakes.

When in the past you may have shouted someone down or demoted someone, VPM calls for you to put your guns back into your holsters and keep them there. Learn how to offer suggestions and changes. Ask questions, offer encouragement, implement training and team changes, but remain clear on demanding performance and commitment.

Accept that the "boss" moniker is no longer applicable and try "coaches" instead. For your frontline employees, encourage them to speak up, offer suggestions on improvements, accept cross training, and communicate their frustration if the business is not moving or responding fast enough to satisfy their needs and concerns.

For those employees who could not, or would not, buy into the new vision, the higher sense of urgency, the demanding goals and objectives, advise them they should exercise their personal choices in life outside the company. All team members need to know that you are serious and committed about instituting change and achieving better business performance and that the business must accomplish nothing less.

When it's all added up, VPM works and will work for you. The set of management tools and the VPM associated structure can unlock the extraordinary energy that is inside every employee of the company and bind them to "their" plans and implementation programs that will improve your business results.

Even more than that, it's a change in what your past leadership practices have been, and it will provide confidence in your employees about your willingness to establish new methods while setting higher levels of performance. You will find it will release extraordinary levels of individual performance across the entire workforce, creating more competitive advantage for the business.

It can be a process and playbook that every business leader can apply and that every employee can understand. It can be used with business teams of 20, 200, 2,000, or higher, to blast beyond any goals they set that will enable your business to compete more successfully in today's new world.

You will learn to search and borrow best practices and ideas from others everywhere you can. Everyone will be encouraged to foster an environment where new ideas bubble up continuously. Much like a surgeon and their operating room teammates who follow certain protocols to assure successful results, so should a business team follow a similar process.

The *takeaways* in this chapter are as follows:

I.   It is necessary to do a thorough financial diagnosis analysis of your business performance needs before you launch or fix your business.

II.   By using the Vision Powered Management structured

process, the analysis of your business and the resulting actions become consistent with your vision statement and business goal.

III.   The process requires high employee involvement whereby the employees determine and agree on the steps needed to achieve improved business results and carry out the solutions.

IV.   It requires the business to adopt and accept a high sense of urgency to get the important things done.

V.   VPM establishes an attitude that numbers on business measures matter and achieving the numbers is a necessity.

CHAPTER 3:

Clearing the Decks

The Vision Powered Management process in sum total is seven steps. Within the initiation of each of the steps, the information generated from each step informs others along the way.

The first six steps discussed in this chapter are aimed at clearing the decks of obstacles of change for any business, new or existing, on its current course. By removing these obstacles, the process allows the creation of a new culture that will foster and readily embrace change.

Step seven, Implement, is just introduced in this chapter, and the complete details are discussed in chapter 4, "Implementation." Most of my discussion is based on experiences associated with overhauling and reinventing an existing business. For the reader who is in the category of starting a new business, think about what aspects of these steps you might adopt and apply to your new business.

There really is no skipping of steps unless you are a new

business. In the case of a new business, step two becomes a matter of simply assessing which buckets your products or services go in to.

Step 1. Establish Financial Ground Rules

This step of the process requires that a business leader select certain financial ground rules to be attained for the business to be successful. The reason for this is that today's global economy is very value driven. No longer can you rest on your laurels with just good products, quality, and service. Being price competitive and being profitable is an absolute necessity. Here are the ground rules I found most useful during my management experiences.

- Be in the top 25 percent of the markets the business serves.

- Achieve year over year sales growth of 15 percent.

- Deliver a minimum profit before tax (PBT) of 15 percent of sales.

- Achieve free cash flow equal to net income, where free cash flow is the money left after all operating and investment expenses are paid.

Other ground rules that could be considered are return on investment, current ratio, debt-to-equity ratio, and the efficiency ratios of inventory turnover and receivables turnover. Perhaps your team provides internal support for areas like customer service or IT support. Key performance indicators such as tickets closed or customer satisfaction survey data can also be used as ground rules. See Appendix 2 for definitions of important financial measurements.

Step 2. **Establish Product Categories**

This step is primarily used for an existing business or team. One needs to evaluate the financial level at which the business has been operating. This should be accomplished quickly where the financial staff provides the most recent three years' operating data for each of the product lines of the business.

The data provided is then matched against the ground rules, including market share, major competitors, sales dollars, and year-over-year % change [V %], PBT $ and V %, free cash flow $ and V %, total cost productivity %, and V % and Return on Investment %.

You will need to analyze the data provided and assign the results into categories. For example, if you provide tech support to external or internal customers, evaluate each of the products or services that come with your team's work. The results of your evaluation of your services or products should then be put in categories.

In my experience working with an industrial products business, I categorized the various products into the following three categories:

- Flat/Declining Revenue, Mature Products: These are usually older products, or services for those products, where the demand is primarily for spare parts and/or service calls.

- Flat/Increasing Revenue, Current Products: Products still being produced and sold to existing and new customers, including spare parts and service support.

- Increasing Revenue, New Growth Products: Products that have been recently introduced for sale with newer technologies, are exhibiting high acceptance rates by existing and new customers, and are enjoying rapid sales growth. In certain situations, these products can be priced higher than normal depending on the degree of ingenuity and originality of them.

Once this is done, the business leader communicates the results of the analysis with his staff, and makes any valid changes needed regarding the product line classifications. Once there is consensus on the results, a financial baseline strategy is established for each of the product lines, as shown in figure 1.

As a new business matures and grows, its products and services can be allocated into these same or similar categories:

Product Lines	Financial Baseline Strategy
Flat/Declining Mature	Maximize profit, cash flow, and productivity with minimum investment.
Flat/Increasing Revenue Current	Meet profit, cash flow, and productivity goals with moderate investment.
Increasing Revenue New	Grow market share, profit, and cash flow and meet productivity goals, supported by required investments

Figure 1.
Financial Baseline Strategy

Step 3. Instigate a Culture of Change

This step encourages instigating change quickly to create a different environment within the business that is inherited. I had to change the industrial products company from one whose fortunes had been in the hands of a few to one that would be driven by the capability of many.

We had to go from medium involvement to high involvement by everyone in the company, marching to a high-speed, numerically defined, and values-driven culture. Change had to be felt across and down the entire organization. People had to buy in to the change process and have a solid understanding of what needed to be done and what the required results for success were that everyone would have to rally around.

The initial change was aimed at urgently improving performance. Most personnel are coming to their jobs every day with good intention. However, in many cases they are not stretching themselves far and hard enough in their jobs. The business leader needs to heighten their focus on the core business issues that need to be improved and those that are going to be paramount to future success.

This business was operating on a monthly rhythm, i.e. critical core business results were being measured and reported monthly. Meetings were held peppered with engineers, accountants, marketers, factory workers etc. In agenda-based meetings I talked about teamwork and training, solving problems and selling solutions, and why it was important to establish and embrace new operating values.

Everything we did had to pass the test of being good for the customer i.e., do it with speed, do it simply, implement the necessary training, knowledge, technology and have the confidence to assure success. Employees were asked how they felt about a conversion from a pure vertical organization, Figure 2, to one with a horizontal team matrix organization overlay on it, Figure 3. I would take notes where employees identified and requested some help or actions to be taken. Emphasis was placed on how important it is to attach numbers to anything you are trying to improve.

Almost everything important in life is measured numerically, whether it be your income, taxes, blood pressure, vehicle speed, time, or budget. If you can't put a number on an action necessary to improve your business performance, it is probably not worth spending much time on it.

Figure 2.
Traditional Vertical Organization

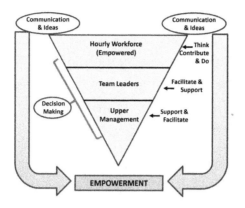

Figure 3.
Horizontal Team Matrix Organization Overlay

I did a lot of walk-arounds through the various work areas, whether it was in product development, marketing or the factory floor areas. I would stop and ask people how things were going, were there any problems they needed help with? If people did not look busy, I would call the supervisor over and ask what the problem might be? What were they were doing about it? and did they need my help to get things resolved more quickly?

In those first several months I traveled frequently to our sales offices to keep them in the loop about the changes and listen to how they felt about our support to their selling efforts. It is important to know if customers are happy or unhappy about how the business is serving their needs. I was looking for disconnects between the performance data that had been provided and the real world of the sales teams dealing with customers. The sales teams are the eyes and ears of the customer base and the best source for signs of needed improvement, and even more importantly, signs of dissatisfaction with the customer base.

The walk arounds, field visits to sales offices and customer meetings, along with the weekly morning meetings, allowed me to continuously monitor the pulse of the business, and to either take comfort in the early progress we were making, or raise some hell where progress was too slow in coming.

On occasion an employee would be encountered who would complain about some of the changes being started. The pattern these employees had in communicating their displeasure was interesting. It usually was a mix of complaint, but not offering any helpful suggestions for improvement. It typically ended with "I don't like what I am hearing and would like things to stay as they are". In other words, "if we would only go back to the previous ways of doing things".

My response was along the lines of, "Please take off those rose-colored glasses that have the rear looking side mirrors on them, get on board this train and the direction we are heading toward. If you are not comfortable in a new, more invigorating environment, perhaps you should consider getting off the train". This may sound harsh to readers but one of the lessons learned is that occasionally an organization needs to hear directly that there is no turning back on the new direction of the business. It needs to be done in a manner where it comes from the top and causes the message to get around the organization quickly.

During this 90-day time period, the business rhythm was changed from monthly reporting to a weekly reporting basis and that weekly business results be on my desk every Monday morning at 7:30 am.

Those weekly results initially would include orders received, sales delivered, cash flow, variable cost %'s to sales, and product margin %'s. Weekly 7:30am group meetings with my direct reports were held to review and discuss the results, establish necessary action items and act on all important items.

A business leader needs to continuously search for areas of performance needing improvement. Examples of areas that you can look at might be market share, percent on time deliveries, warranty expense, inventory turnover, aging of receivables, and manufacturing cycle times. At the close of every meeting it is necessary to assign someone to take on the task of making improvement happen urgently while measuring progress along the way.

During this early time period it was necessary to rapidly streamline the existing organization. Today's information revolution is acting like a time bomb being dropped on a vertical hierarchical organization. Information must reach those closest to the work as quickly as possible and not go through a litany of steps, places or filtering on its way.

In my opinion, any hierarchical organization structures that still exist must be flattened, or more popularly known as delayered. The traditional power base of the bureaucrat, the possession of information only known to the "higher ups", needs to be stripped away. Information must move thru a vertical organization chain of command quickly to the point where it is needed most.

Organizations typically have 5 layers of management, from the top CEO, to Functional Sections such as Marketing, Sales, Engineering, Manufacturing, Human Relations, etc., to Subsections, to Units, to Operations within each of the Functional Sections. The VPM Process requires that the number of vertical sections of the organization be reduced to a minimum. Approval levels need not only be assigned by financial needs but also by moving them close to the point of work. It recommends that closely related vertical work functions be melded together instead of standing alone.

For example, Human Resources and Legal may be combined, Sales and Marketing combined, Technology and Manufacturing combined, etc. Horizontal organization levels need to be eliminated by increasing the spans of each level. This needs to be top down driven and accomplished very quickly.

For example, if the business currently has 5 layers from the factory or office floor to the top, get it to 3. It is very important that these tasks are done on an accelerated basis to demonstrate to the organization that change is a high priority and that the business is to perform on an accelerated rhythm going forward.

Once the delayering is done, the next step is to push approval levels for expenditures, hiring decisions, promotions, etc. to the organization levels that are closest to where the work is done. In addition, co-locating team employees with decision authority is much more efficient than having them separated in vertical organization chimneys.

In many cases, by investing in new software systems and training, computers can be used to assist in work planning, tracking results, time records, work assignments and the like, reducing the increased time burdens on coaches driven by the delayering of the organization.

It is when step three is implemented and, on its way, that cultural changes start to be felt through the organization.

Step 4. Streamline the Organization

This step is taken to remove and disallow bureaucracy. This is done by embarking on an effort to identify procedural rules and procedures that cause either unnecessary work to be done, or cumbersome approvals to be in hand before work can proceed.

In other words, get rid of "junk work" as quickly as possible. It would make no sense to try to raise the performance level of employees if at the same time the business was requiring tasks that were no longer necessary.

Examples of potentially unnecessary work would be meetings, multiple levels of approval, reports and policies that have become routine and out of date. By eliminating unproductive activities, it frees up and allows employee energy to be applied to areas needing improvement. Streamlining necessitates that every function in the business must be intolerant of non-essential work.

It's a Declaration of War on:

- Non-essential work
- Non-essential meetings
- Non-essential measurements
- Non-essential policies
- Non-essential approvals

Ted Levitt, a past Editor of the Harvard Business Review, once said "Nothing is more wasteful than doing with great efficiency that which should not be done anymore". Every business function should periodically examine these areas and determine if they are necessary to continue as part of their business practices, and if not, change or eliminate them.

Take meetings as an example. Salary.com did a survey regarding meetings. "Too many meetings" was identified as the top timewaster cited by 47% of those surveyed. Think about imposing rules on meetings such as: allot a 48-minute maximum time, require written agendas that list the subject matter, identify the clear goals of the meeting and include any questions that will be asked. Think about removing chairs and having stand up meetings.

Streamline the Bureaucracy

Reports

Approvals

Meetings

Measurements

Policies

25% Are Junk Work

Regarding policies and reports, key questions to ask are as follows:

- Does it serve our customer?
- Does anyone really feel it is a necessary item currently?
- Does it cause any action to be taken?
- Does it contribute to profitability?

If the answers are no, then it is most likely junk work and should be quickly changed or eliminated. By doing so, employees can then use the time that was spent on those activities to work on more productive tasks.

For example, if you have 300 employees and you eliminate

20 minutes a day of junk work for each, it is equivalent to approximately 10-12 more people that can work on productive tasks.

Step 5. Declare Operating Values

The goal of this step is to require the company to identify and pursue specific operating values that will serve to embrace change in its culture. The goal is to develop a business culture that is restless, enjoys striving for improvement, desires growth, wants to be the best at what it does and wants to endlessly build its future.

What might be an example of this? At an Aerospace business that I managed, we held several values and made everything about serving those values extremely important. For example, speed in serving the customer was one of our primary values.

George Stalk Jr. was a Senior Advisor for The Boston Consulting Group, as well as an Adjunct Professor of Strategic Management at the University of Toronto. He was famous for his oft repeated quote, "Time is today's most important competitive weapon of choice".

We used the term AOG in that business. It stood for Aircraft on the Ground. It meant that we had just received an urgent notice that an airplane, military or commercial, was on the ground, unable to take off because a product of ours was found defective during final checkoff. We imposed a rule that required we ship by air a replacement product no later than 4 hours from receipt of the notice.

Sometimes if we did not have a replacement in our warehouse, we either had to produce a new one or contact another customer to see if they had one that they could make available. Once we had the needed product, we shipped directly to the aircraft in distress by the quickest way possible. It was a no excuses rule and it created a sense of extreme urgency in the building that was remarkable.

For my readers, think through your business activities and make a list of those values that are critical for your success, then build a sense of urgency into your business rhythm that assures fulfillment of those values.

Another value that we embraced in that business was simplicity. It is a value to embrace since it contributes to speed by determining the fewest steps necessary to achieve a desired result.

Others to consider are lower cost, product quality and clarity of purpose. It's a win if your team can develop these values since it leads to buy in. If you don't see a value that resonates above, you might consider efficiency, training, curiosity, risk taking, trust, honesty, mutual respect and transparency in how the company conducts its business operations.

Step 6. Empower the Employees

This step involves teaching ALL personnel about the concept of empowerment. Empowerment is the act of granting the power, right, or authority to perform various acts or duties. It is the idea that giving employees skills, resources, authority, opportunity, and motivation, it contributes to their overall competence, happiness, and confidence, and results in higher overall productivity.

In many of my early assignments, managers turned time and

time again to a select group under their leadership when matters required urgent solutions to problems. In your own situations, when you encounter a significant challenge in your business, how do you react to getting the problem resolved? Do you turn time after time to the same people to get a solution in place? Are you reluctant to entrust others to get the job done? When the time pressures are important do you feel that only the "crack" team can get the job done?

If your answers are yes to these questions, then implementing ways to have more of your employees accept empowerment will result in higher levels of the overall productivity of your business. In most cases it is helpful to hire specialists in the field to come into the business and conduct training courses for all employees so that the employee base has more skills, self-confidence, and willingness to take on challenging assignments.

Think about establishing a classroom specifically dedicated to teaching employees about topics such as empowerment, how to identify and solve problems, how to identify alternative solutions, how to identify stakeholders, i.e. those who would be affected by and involved in a change in process, how to gain "buy in" from the stakeholders of changes, and what the benefits of cross train-ing are both for them and the business.

As an example of teaching the benefits of cross training to em-ployees we used analogies to the sports world. The conversation would go something like this. Imagine each of you is a member of a coed basketball team. You were interviewed and hired for a job based on your qualifications. Mary was hired for the position of guard based on her height of 5' 9", speed, her ability to dribble and pass the ball. John was hired as the center of the team because he was 6′ 11″, he was physically strong, a great jumper for the tipoff and rebounds, and a good inside shooter.

One more guard and two forwards were hired based on the qualifications for those positions. The coach of the team would teach all the players certain additional skills they would find beneficial to their ability to win games. We pointed out to the employees that the basketball players were "hired" just like them for their specific qualifications and skills. We then would say, just visualize a situation where the opposing team just took a shot and missed. John is around the basket but has been boxed out by the opposing team and can't get to the rebound. Mary quickly elbows her way through and grabs the rebound and makes a long pass down the court to one of their forwards who stuffs the ball in for a basket.

This was a situation where John who was hired to get rebounds could not perform his required task. Mary did not stand around criticizing John, she jumped in and helped. Rebounding was one of the skills that the coach taught all the players. The coach knew that winning requires that everyone do their very best to act together to maximize success on the job. Mary knew instantly that she had rebounding skills, she was empowered by the coach to use the skill and had the self-confidence to do it.

We then would ask the employees how they would react if a task came up that was someone else's job. Didn't it make sense that cross training employees would make a team performance stronger and better? Most people relate well to team-based sports so analogies like this are helpful teaching aids on subjects involving behavioral change, like empowerment and cross training.

Step 7. Implement

This step is the most time consuming and challenging part of the VPM process. I'm going to just introduce the components of this step here as I wind up this chapter. Creating a Vision Statement means embarking on a process in which the employees participate in creating a brief sentence or two that declares what the purpose of the business is that they want to embrace and adopt.

People sometimes have difficulty in understanding the difference between vision and mission statements. The word mission in my mind speaks more to the short term, is focused on more singular objectives and is tactical in nature. Vision, an elusive word, is language that describes a picture of what the future is to be like. In this sense it connotes permanence because its futurity assures a long-lasting pursuit. It identifies significance and priority of matters that should stand the test of time but also embraces flexibility.

Another way to think about it is that it describes the purpose and the basic reason[s] for the business's existence. The elements of a Vision Statement are further elaborated on in Figure 1. The Vision Powered Management Process then proceeds beyond the Statement and encompasses many sustaining change steps to embed throughout the business that are necessary to sustain success over the longer term.

Once the employees have engaged and adopted a Vision Statement, the process then requires setting one overall business goal. There is one overall business goal in my experience that should be adopted and that is "Satisfy Customers Profitably".

My dumbed downed reasoning for this is as follows. Customer dollars spent on products brings cash into the business. The total cost of those sales, subtracted from the Customer purchase price, less equipment costs, results in free cash, or real profit, available for the business to spend on other important items.

In its simplest terms free cash flow is the lifeblood of the business. As with a human being, if you run out of blood you die. A business, if it assumes too much debt, and does not generate enough free cash flow to support reducing its debt and the expense needs of its business, it also faces imminent death.

For example, it hinders the ability of the business to respond to marketplace changes, such as newer technology products and new competitors, and/or to adequately service its debt, thereby endangering its future. Some once successful businesses that lost their way that come to mind are Westinghouse, Chrysler, Sears, RCA, and my Alma Mater, GE. Tesla, the electric car maker is struggling now, overburdened with debt, not generating anywhere near the free cash flow it needs and facing the possibility of reorganization under bankruptcy in order to continue operations.

Once the Vision and Business goal is adopted, the business begins to address the task of identifying the most important areas of the business needing improvement, or development, as in the case of a new business. This includes prioritizing the order of attack, defining objectives, strategies, implementation tactics and measurements that the highly involved work teams can implement to achieve the desired improvements.

To be successful in this implementation endeavor, it is necessary to unlock the minds, energy and commitment of every employee and then have them "sign up" for the necessary improvement or development steps. Keep in mind that just like any initiative, the benefit doesn't just happen when you get the result. The "real benefit" here or "medicine" is discovered by your employees inside the process of following a pathway of prescribed implementation steps. As your teams take these steps together, they find their way to improved levels of performance.

During the period in which visits to the sales offices occurred and the operating speed of the business increased, the Human Relations head coach was asked to assemble a group of employees to develop and define a Vision Statement. The team was to be led by a highly respected business member who had experience in several functions of the business. This individual also had to have demonstrated strength in consensus building. Once the team was formed, they were instructed to brainstorm and provide a response in 45 days to each of the following items:

1. Provide in a single sentence what the purpose of the business needed to be and include an overriding goal for the business to strive at achieving.

2. Identify the top areas of the business needing improvement. For example, such areas as reducing the elapsed time for new product introductions, reduce manufacturing cycle times, improve shipment promises kept, improve product quality levels, etc.

3. Include personnel in the group from every function of the business such as manufacturing, engineering, marketing,

sales, service, and finance. It's important when doing this to purposely include "influencers" in the process. "Influencers" are people who are highly respected for their knowledge and performance in their own functional segments as well as peer organization segments.

4. The areas identified as needing improvement must be forward looking and include stated objectives to be achieved. Each of the business functions such as engineering, marketing, manufacturing, etc., must identify steps to be taken in their areas that will contribute to the improved performance. All steps to be taken must include specific numerically defined actions that must be achieved.

5. Identify behavior values that the business should adopt and foster to guide the conduct of every member of the business and the company's actions.

6. Include recommended rewards and celebration ideas for achieved success along the way. Rewards could include a group bonus, a company-wide celebration party, Key Performer awards such as a night out for dinner with spouse or friend, etc.

7. Include ideas on how best to communicate the results of the process to the employee base as a means of achieving buy-in to the Vision process results, such as a graded report card, dashboards, newsletter, etc.

8. Include recommendations on how best to change the organization modus operandi from a vertical functional base to a horizontal overlay multi-functional team base, sometimes referred to as a matrix base.

The output from this assignment would form the basis for the next step of the Vision Powered Management process, which is covered in Chapter 4, Implementation.

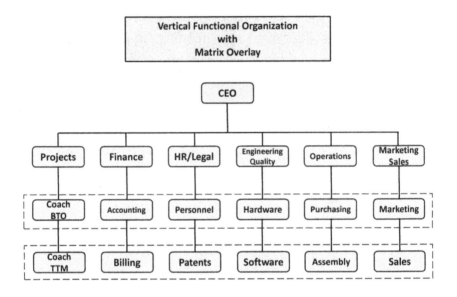

The **takeaways** from this chapter are as follows;

I.   Establish Operating ground rules for the business to focus its activities on. Q: What will your ground rules be for your team/ unit / business?

II.   When taking on a business or creating one, make certain you emphasize doing work in a fast and efficient manner that results in more competitiveness, lower costs, higher profitability, and better cash flow. Q: In what areas do you see opportunities for improvement?

III. Create a culture in the business that fosters eliminating all unnecessary activities to focus employee activity on just meaningful work. Q: In what ways can you foster the culture necessary for eliminating these activities? Can you create a bounty for anyone that finds an activity that can be trimmed away?

IV.   Create an employee developed vision that states the real purpose of the business and that results in most everyone coming together to support a common set of values and practices; all centered on business success. Q: Who might you appoint in a cross functional team to drive this vision process? What are the timelines?

V.   Conduct activities in the most simple and easy to understand way. This means taking the fewest number of steps in a procedure, design the product with the fewest parts, write service manuals with the fewest words, use illustrations where possible instead of words, etc. as a means of achieving better performance. Q: Have you highlighted to your employees the simple slogan, "the simpler the better"?

VI.   Foster empowerment and cross training to enable more employees to willingly jump in and help when log jams occur. Q: How can you consistently support the building of coaches on your team to encourage the spirit of helping, not criticizing, when an obstacle occurs?

VII. Create values of telling the truth all the time, treating others with respect, being good listeners, helping others, enjoying challenges, being a contributing team member, and exercising empowerment to encourage all employees to run on all cylinders.

CHAPTER 4:

Implementation

The implementation phase of Vision Powered Management is depicted in Figure 1. The process begins with the creation of a Vision Statement and Overall Business Goal, both of which were discussed in Chapter 3. Here are some Vision statements from notable companies as a means of providing some insight into what a statement could include. They are as follows:

Apple

> "We believe that we are on the face of the earth to make great products and that's not changing. We are constantly focusing on innovating. We believe in the simple not the complex. We believe that we need to own and control the primary technologies behind the products that we make and participate only in markets where we can make a significant contribution. We believe in saying no to thousands of projects, so that we can really focus on the few that are truly important and meaningful to us. We

believe in deep collaboration and cross-pollination of our groups, which allow us to innovate in a way that others cannot. And frankly, we don't settle for anything less than excellence in every group in the company, and we have the self-honesty to admit when we're wrong and the courage to change. And I think regardless of who is in what job those values are so embedded in this company that Apple will do extremely well."

Google

"To provide access to the world's information in one click."

GE

"To become the world's premier digital industrial company, transforming industry with software-defined machines and solutions that are connected, responsive and predictive."

Amazon

"Be earth's most customer-centric company, to build a place where people can come to find and discover anything they might want to buy online."

Starbucks

"To inspire and nurture the human spirit – one person, one cup, and one neighborhood at a time."

Disney

"To make people happy."

Charles Schwab

"Helping investors help themselves."

LinkedIn

"To connect the world's professionals and make them more productive and successful."

As you can see, all except Apple have one sentence Vision statements. All except Apple are focused externally, and all describe a long-lasting purpose. Apple's statement is really a mission statement, focused internally, very tactical in nature and not easily remembered.

GE's statement is more of a mission statement as well. To aspire to be the "world's premium digital industrial company utilizing digital technology and software applications to enhance the performance of one's products" is describing implementation tactics as opposed to creating an externally customer focused vision.

The balance of the statements were valid and interesting vision statements. Here are some tips that may be helpful to those who want to create a vision statement for their business.

It should be worded in a way that people want to act, to overcome obstacles, and put real effort into achieving. It should fit with your business activity, culture and history. It needs to be inclusive by including your personnel and your customers. It should be challenging yet achievable. Last it should be clear to understand and be readily communicated.

A company can be successful for a variety of reasons and the Vision statement is just one part of the process of success. It is a very important starting point because it is a constant reminder of why you are in business. The VPM process requires having employees of the company participate in that process, to avoid it being perceived as just a top down driven PR statement. Why? because the Vision becomes theirs, not just management's, and they buy into it.

As you recall from Chapter 3 a cross functional team was charged to create a Vision statement and overall Business Goal for the GE Industrial business. Here is the statement and goal that emerged from that activity:

> **Vision Statement**: "To improve the productivity of our Customers by providing them the best technology, reliability and services worldwide."

> **Business Goal**: "Satisfy Customers Profitably."

Numerous things struck me immediately. First, the vision was focused externally on the customer and how we needed to support and improve their businesses. Second, we had to raise the level of providing our products and services to be the "best" available. Third, we had to expand our involvement in markets outside of the Americas, hence the word worldwide. Fourth, we had to emphasize long term quality hence the selection of the word reliability.

Our team members defined a purpose for the business they felt was worthwhile. A purpose they could commit to and one which they felt good about. Also, they seconded my recommended overall business goal of "Satisfy Customers Profitably". By doing so our team members recognized we were in business to satisfy customers and by doing so the profits would flow.

I felt we were on the way to success. We had a vision statement that people believed in, we had a specific business overall goal to achieve, and we had identified areas of the business to become the best. The high rate of involvement and acceptance by the employee team signified that they realized their future success would rest upon how well everyone would have to contribute to the improvement of both our customer's and our own business results.

We proceeded to make banners of the Vision Statement and the business goal and placed them all over the facilities – cafeteria, hallways, visitor entrance, office locations, etc. – to keep them constantly in the minds of the employees.

Next is the effort to identify and prioritize the most important actions that the business should implement on the pathway to become the best. This is where the really challenging, rewarding and time-consuming work begins, i.e. the act of improving what is needed to be improved.

We had created a basket of items that needed to improve from the ideas that came out of "clearing the decks", such as the Sales force feedback from customers, outdated procedures and processes to mention just a few. The team was asked to provide a structured process for implementing change to assure that it gets embedded in a timely fashion throughout the business, that it keeps track of what has been done and what remains to be done.

The structure framework used by the team is discussed next and shown in Figure 1.

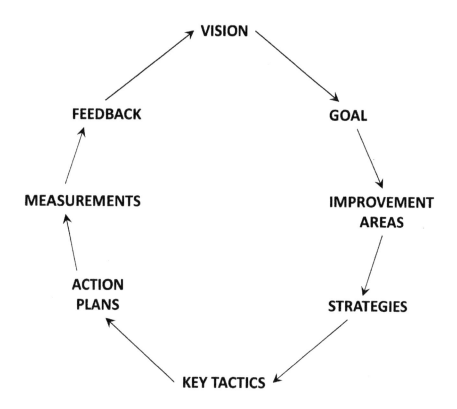

Figure 1.
VPM Implementation Structure Framework

1. VISION STATEMENT

   To improve our customer's productivity with the best product technology, reliability and service worldwide.

2. BUSINESS GOAL

To satisfy customers' requirements profitably.

3. PRIMARY AREAS NEEDING IMPROVEMENT

The Areas selected were Customer Satisfaction, Product Leadership, Revenue Growth and Reliability.

4. STRATEGIES

The team selected the Customer Satisfaction and Product Leadership Areas as the initial ones that should be targeted. The Customer Satisfaction implementation strategy selected was to reduce the order to ship time cycle. The Product Leadership implementation strategy was shortening the new product introduction time cycle. Those strategies are then passed on to the various cross functional teams doing product manufacturing and product design who then develop the tactics and action plans to achieve the strategies.

5. TACTICS

The tactics to be employed were 1. Customer satisfaction: institute a new build to order system [BTO] that would replace a build to marketing forecast system. The benefit of a new BTO would reduce the manufacturing cycle time, and implement a Pareto based finished goods inventory for high use products to improve shipment promises kept PK %.

[A Pareto Analysis is based on the theory that 30% of the products produced account for 70% of the customer orders.] 2. Product Leadership: Implement new approaches and technologies for product design that would shorten the time when they would be available for sale to customers, in short reduce "Time to Market" [TTM].

6. ACTIONS

    Detailed action plans and schedules must be established and implemented in support of the Tactics. These tasks become the responsibility of the senior functional coaches of the business, and the cross functional horizontal teams.

7. MEASUREMENTS

    Identify key measurements to monitor progress against stated goals contained in the action plans. For example, for the Customer Satisfaction actions, Cycle Time from order to ship in weeks and Promises Kept [PK%] became the key measures. For Product Leadership, TTM in weeks was selected.

8. COMMUNICATING

    Monthly all employee Operating Reviews were established, and Head Coaches of functions reported on the status of the action plans.

An important aspect of the VPM process is to establish a rule that the implementation teams should only tackle two or three primary items at a time that the business needs to improve. Otherwise the change process gets distracted and mired down trying to improve too many items at once. By following the rule, once the initial items are implemented, teams are required to take on the next two or three. In simple terms, over time the VPM process morphs into a continuous improvement methodology.

One last point. There is a lot of thinking out in industry that believes people-system improvements, or technology investments by themselves, can be the key to future success. As you will see in reading through details of the action plans the truth is that you must do both wisely in order to succeed in this increasingly complex and globalized market. Remember, nothing good comes easy!

The teams responsible for the actions were instructed to implement the prescribed tactics on an urgent basis. As the CEO Head Coach, the teams were given the following challenges. First, reduce the cycle time from customer orders received to shipment date from an average of 6 weeks to 2 weeks and to meet shipment promise dates 100 % of the time. Secondly, reduce the time to introduce new products to market in half, from an average of 18 months to 9 months. The teams were also asked to consider the following questions as they proceeded on their paths of implementation:

- How can costs be reduced or at least held constant in the face of increasing product and process complexity?

- How can a rapid response to customer orders be maintained when inventories must be reduced in order to generate acceptable levels of cash flow?

- How can design times be reduced when products must incorporate more and more embedded intelligence, i.e., be smarter and at the same time be simpler?

- How can material handling and manufacturing processes be sped up while maintaining flexibility to accommodate building to order?

I was making the point that just focusing on speed was not necessarily going to provide the right results. One of the skills that a good leader uses is to use questions instead of barking commands all the time. Questions tend to stimulate people to factor in surrounding matters prior to pursuing a specific path to a solution. The phrase "thinking out of the box" points in this same direction. Too much barking can turn a person's brain off.

Returning to the discussion of the structure, here are the implementation TACTICS chosen by the Build to Order team:

- Implement a new best in class Order Ship and Bill [OSB] software system that generates upon receipt the necessary manufacturing and invoicing information by order received.

- Focus on similarity of processes versus dissimilarities of products.

- Install a new automated components parts and finished goods warehousing system.

- Install a 3 shift robotic assembly area.

- Create point of use inventories at assembly areas.

- Employ parallel vs. serial manufacturing processes.

ACTIONS TAKEN – BUILD TO ORDER [BTO]

The previous Order, Ship and Bill [OSB] system was designed to support a build to marketing forecast system which were popular at that time. Most of those systems would wind up with inventory problems and long delivery cycles due to the fundamental inaccuracies associated with forecasting the unknown.

This occurs because of some products enjoying much higher demand and some suffering much lower demand than forecasted. The resulting shortages of the component parts needed by the more salable products cause schedule delays and inventory problems with too many low demand products sitting in finished inventory.

At the same time, you can be tying up manufacturing facilities building products at higher rate than anyone is going to purchase. If marketers could predict the future accurately, they would be in the stock market business instead. Just look at weather forecasting if you are a fan of forecasts. Throwing the old system away and implementing a Build to Order system was the correct path to take.

The automated parts warehouse had two major objectives, the first being that high-volume part suppliers would bypass our receiving area and deliver directly to the stock bins designated for the items purchased from them. This eliminated our receiving personnel having to unpack, move and stock them in the correct bins. When stock levels approached minimum levels due to assembly usage, emails were sent to those suppliers advising they had to restore them to the initial stock levels.

By thinking out of the box we saved both time and money. Parts were retrieved automatically from their respective bins and delivered to the newly created point of use inventory areas when needed. In that way we eliminated any waiting time on the part of the assembly personnel.

By investing in robotic assembly stations, we could run three shifts a day instead of one shift because there was no longer a person involved in the assembly process. In many respects the robots resembled a group of praying mantises moving 24/7 all the time.

Finally, we converted manufacturing multiple operation assembly areas from being serial based to parallel based. In serial operation a batch of 60 items going through 3 operations at 1 minute per operation would take 180 minutes to complete. Under parallel processing the lot size of 60 is broken down into 3 sets of 20 items, each set being completed in 60 minutes done in parallel.

After the first operation of Set 1 is completed, set 2 starts operation 1 and Set 3 starts operation 1 right after Set 2 completes operation 1. This results in the three sets being completed in 100 minutes total, a 44% reduction in cycle time. See Parallel vs. Sequential productions shown in Figure 2. The BTO project was completed in 18 months and in the first full year cycle time was cut in half, down to 3 weeks, a 50% reduction.

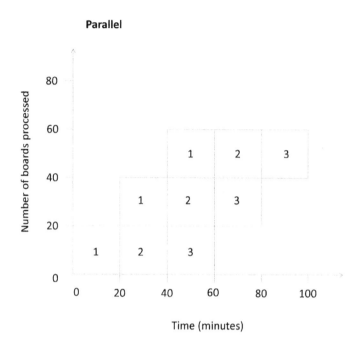

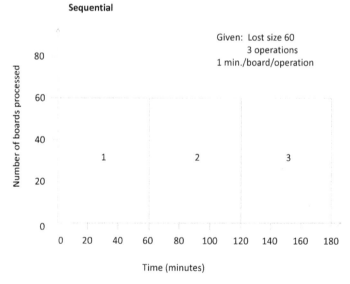

Figure 2.
Parallel vs. Sequential Production

Here are the TACTICS chosen by the Product Leadership team to achieve cutting the time to market [TTM] for new products by 50% from an average of 18 months to 9 months. The cross functional team recognized that this cycle time had to be drastically reduced if we were to be the best of the best. They had to mobilize the product developers around three major themes, employ world class computer-based design technologies, take advantage of historical hardware and software design solutions, and integrate downstream processes, such as product testing programs and technical publications, needed as part of finalizing product release for sale to customers.

ACTIONS TAKEN – TIME TO MARKET [TTM]

The team spent a considerable amount of time reviewing the latest offerings from the major suppliers of computer aided engineering design solutions. Once they narrowed down to their preferred choice, they advised the supplier that as part of their final contract, the supplier would have to provide two of their installation experts to become part of our in-house team. In this way the implementation cycle would proceed much faster by having questions being answered on the spot, accelerating the time of implementation. Another example of thinking out of the box.

Next the team developed a library of reusable circuit designs from earlier products that could be selected for new products. Similarly, they developed a library of reusable existing software function blocks for use in a new design. These two initiatives could account for as much as 40% of the time spent on a new product design. New design workstations were purchased for the designers in order to take advantage of these new methods.

Next, they addressed mechanical design cycle time required for tooling needs and the need for early prototypes. Stereo lithography, a new process using 3D computer model design coupled with laser and photopolymers, could be used to create soft tooling and soft prototype mechanical models in days. This eliminated the need to create formal drawings, receive bids and outsource the work to make hard models that would typically take 6-8 weeks. In simpler terms, Art to Part in days versus weeks.

Finally, since most of the products were electronic based, designs were handed off to the Quality Control team so they could develop software programs for their factory automatic test equipment. By using new computer aided design workstations those programs would become an output of the design process, eliminating that handoff step, another time and cost saver. By co-locating the technical publications team with the design team, the publications were done in parallel with the design cycle, another time saver.

The TTM process was implemented over a 22-month period and resulted in improved design quality, and it reduced the number of design iterations in half. In the first year, new design to market times were reduced by a third, from 18 months to 12 months. This was equivalent to having 1/3 more engineers on the payroll designing new products. The following year the cycle was down to 11. The company was awarded the award for Excellence in Computer Aided Engineering by CAE Magazine. It was a finalist for the best TTM process for Concurrent Engineering from Machine Design Magazine. More importantly we had satisfied a part of the Vision by becoming one of the best technology companies at that time.

The action plans implemented in this very first phase using the VPM structure are summarized in Figure 3.

Build to Order [BTO] Team A

- Parallel vs. Serial Production
- New Build to Order software system [BTO]
- Create Point of Use Inventories
- Automate parts warehousing
- Create Express Manufacturing area
- 3 shift Robotic parts Assembly

Reduce Time to Market [TTM] Team B

- Create Reusable Design Library
- Create Reusable Software Function blocks
- 3D laser tooling
- 3D laser prototyping
- Computer generated testing programs

Figure 3.
Action Plan Summary

Once the teams completed this initial set of strategies, they moved on to expanding our market reach by taking on the global expansion and reliability parts of the Vision statement. Two strategies were selected, the first to create a sales presence in the rapidly developing Asia Pacific region and second to install a world class business wide quality system directed at improving the reliability of the company's products.

With respect to the Asia Pacific tactic, the team focused on creating a sales force presence in each of the major markets. A headquarters operation with a sales office was established in Singapore. Additional sales offices were established in Kuala Lumpur, Malaysia, Bangkok, Thailand, Bandung, Indonesia, Bangalore, India, Beijing, Shenzhen and Shanghai, China. This was accomplished in 16 months including recruiting personnel, renting facilities, product training, manual translations to local languages and training in our company methods and values. Over the next 3 years sales in those areas grew rapidly.

In the early 90's the International Standards Organization [ISO] began a campaign to have companies adopt a new publication ISO 9000, a guideline for quality management and quality assurance system. The guideline established methods for documenting and maintaining an effective quality assurance system as a means of demonstrating to customers your ability to supply high quality products.

ISO 9000 was a global nation to nation standard. It went largely unnoticed in the U.S. for quite a few years. U.S. headquartered companies that had an international presence became aware of it when large European utility and petrochemical businesses required their suppliers to be registered as conforming to it as a condition of doing business.

The U.S. National Electrical Manufacturers Association began to promote it in the U.S. as it became more and more accepted in the European market as a 'must have". In order to be registered as in compliance, a business had to meet the requirements of the conformance subset titled ISO 9001. ISO 9001 was the most comprehensive conformance document one could imagine.

The team recommended, and the head coaches agreed, to embark on a pathway to achieve conformance in support of the vision to be the best in reliability, which is quality over time. Because of the importance of this task the Quality Head Coach was assigned to be the cross functional team leader and we proceeded toward achieving conformance. This process required documentation of many informal procedures that existed in Marketing, Sales and Design, improved equipment calibration rigors, and frequent internal audits of our compliance to these requirements.

After 14 months of work and 10 days of independent audit, we became the first U.S. company to be registered as in compliance with ISO 9001. Another milestone was achieved along the way of becoming the best of the best, powered by the Vision Statement and driven by implementation structure. By now the Vision Powered Management process was embedded in the business and continuous improvement was well underway.

Take-aways from this Chapter are as follows;

I. Create a Vision Statement for your business no matter its size. It will serve to steer you and your employees along a common pathway for success. Have employees participate in the process so it becomes a shared vision.

II. Highlight the necessity to achieve profitability by including that as the Business Goal. Remember companies begin to die when they do not regularly generate free cash flow.

III. Utilize cross functional employees to help identify areas of the business needing improvement and recruit them to identify and implement solutions. Always remember, those closest to the work know best what can be improved.

IV. Train your employees to recognize the benefit of empowerment and create an environment for teams to become fixers of problems. Teach them analysis skills, problem solving methods, communication skills, and to have a thirst for cross training. Encourage them to become team members and to accept coaching from senior members of the organization.

V. Utilize a structured method for teams to use in approaching problems, defining solutions and implementing actions.

VI. Remember to ask questions at times in lieu of issuing orders as a means of encouraging teams to consider "out of the box" ideas.

VII. Strive to create an environment of continuous improvement in which the employees constantly strive to solve problems as a means of moving the business along a path of becoming the best of the best.

CHAPTER 5:

How you know it's working

As in any endeavor one embarks on, whether it be personal like building a house, losing weight, running a marathon, or a business striving to achieve higher levels of progress, there must be defined goals. The definition of desired levels of achievement, steps to be taken to achieve results and a timetable to measure progress or lack thereof are proven methods for getting anything accomplished. By doing so you set about the engine that is The Vision Powered Management process.

While we discussed the structure of VPM in chapter 4, we will focus on the final steps of the process as well as the measuring and communication aspects in this chapter.

In the many times I utilized the VPM process, the measurement and reporting methods were key components to success. I found that utilizing a familiar and easy to understand method allowed people to quickly understand the results, especially if they would have used it in their everyday lives at one time or another.

The system used had to be communicated regularly with easy to understand results. It also had to address any areas not yet meeting their established goals and provide an explanation of steps being taken to overcome problems encountered. It also required a forecast of their completion dates, and to look for ways to consolidate measurements being used by the various teams on their activities.

The initial methodology selected was using a Report Card format. It was familiar to every employee as nearly everyone had experience with earning a grade. Like report cards, which had to be shared with parents, ours would be shared with all employees so that everyone would know how things were progressing.

A Business Level Report Card [BLRC] was created to measure actual results versus established goals. We measured results such as: Orders Received, Sales Delivered, Profitability, Cash Flow, Inventory Turns, Delivery Promises Kept, Quality Cost as a % to Sales, BTO Cycle Time in Weeks, and TTM Cycle Time in Weeks. Each measurement item received a grade in report card lingo of A's through F's, where anything less than a B was considered underperforming. See the Report Card example in the Appendix.

The report card was reviewed during our all employee meetings named "Operations Reviews". Team members presented the grades, discussed task status and if applicable, what was being done to improve the grade along with the expected timing of project completion vs. timing. Employees were encouraged to ask questions or make suggestions regarding additional improvement ideas. Meetings were held to 55 minutes.

In this way everyone knew if the process was making a difference and whether we were making progress at a good enough pace. It also provided employees the ability to interact with people not normally seen by them in the daily process of getting their jobs done so it was enforcing the horizontal organization transition.

We posted the Report Card in highly visible areas of the business, such as the cafeteria, hallways, entrances and exits to illustrate the urgency and the importance of successful implementation of the Vision process. A clock with the second hand running at twice the speed of a normal clock was installed to signify the importance of running the business at a faster rhythm level than normal. Speed of operating the business is one of the values of VPM.

As time went on, we added additional reporting methods using dashboard type displays such as you have in your car. Once we completed a project, we would set our sights on the next most important one.

Approximately 14 months into the VPM process at one of our Operations Review meetings an employee raised her hand and asked me how everyone would know whether the company was achieving the expected success from the changes implemented. Her question caught me off guard and I hesitated as I struggled with how to answer her. After what seemed to be an eternity to me, I replied "First you and I see the report card at our Operations Reviews showing the grades and the status of how the various projects and business results are faring. As you have seen we are already achieving good progress in each of the measurement areas. In addition to that I will know by the smiles on your faces".

My point was that all of us were going to be the happy recipients of the success that this new way was now beginning to deliver to the business. I knew that what really counted was a high degree of employee participation in achieving higher sales, profits, free cash flow, on time deliveries, higher quality and the like. In other words, the basic factors of success in managing a business would not change, but the ways in which the business goes about achieving that success would, and in our case, had changed, and quite dramatically.

We were already enjoying higher sales, profits, and cash flow. Enthusiastic teamwork, coaching instead of barking orders, and faster deliveries to customers were off to a good start. The workforce recognized that this was occurring because of their efforts and they were very happy about it. As I looked at her and around the auditorium there were a lot more nods and smiling faces than in the past.

You also know it is working when you see more people empowered, implementing improvements, doing what they believe is right, asking for help, listening, searching for answers, and working as a team member. In addition, there will be less people doing only what they are told to do, seeking permission, unwilling to take some risk, complaining instead of solving, and looking upward for answers.

It didn't take a genius to figure out that employees liked the new way better than the old. The new way amounted to a conduit to real involvement. It provided the ability for them to contribute directly to the team's success and empowered their sense of autonomy.

By now the conversion from cops to coaches had occurred and we had streamlined the organization. We were operating with horizontal functional teams in most areas. Tactics were being implemented by the VPM teams for the Build to Order [BTO] and the Time to Market [TTM] teams.

The readers will recall that the initial VPM team established a menu of celebration of success things to do that would be funded by the business. Examples included team parties after work, theater tickets, fitness club special membership promotions, after work softball games, cafeteria cake and coffee parties. As time went on and more successes were happening, the head coaches began to encourage team coaches and functional leaders to recognize the triggers for further celebrations.

We also highlighted successes in the Operations Review. As the coaches learned to celebrate our successes, the team members felt a reinforcement and recognition that it was their efforts driving those improvements.

We embraced and practiced our values of telling the truth and treating each other with respect. The Vision statement was well embedded into our lives and we fostered the concepts of speed, simplicity and confidence in everything we did. Many of our employees had received training in business economics, statistical quality control, computer skills, problem solving techniques, new automated design technologies, art to part mechanical models using 3D laser technology, and high-speed data networks.

Five years from the initiation of the Vision Powered Management process we achieved the following results:

- Sales growth of 5 times our starting level of $100 Million. This is a 37.5% AAGR.

- Pretax profit of 15%.

- Inventory turns from 4 to 12.

- Free cash flow equaled net income.

- BTO time from 12 weeks to 3.

- TTM time from 18 months to 11.

- Cost of product failures 0.6% to sales.

- Total employment increased 21%.

It may sound like I'm bragging on our success, and you'll pardon me for tooting our employees' horn further. We received some prestigious awards acknowledging our successes driven by the VPM process. I was especially proud of the following three awards:

- "Manufacturing Excellence Award" from _Controls and Systems Engineering Magazine_ for "superior product quality, degree of design integration, degree of manufacturing automation, concurrent engineering processes, ongoing employee training and focus on customer commitment".

- _Electronics Business Magazine_ awarded us with their "Electronics Factory Automation Award" under the categories of "best use of new manufacturing technology to cut costs, increase quality and enhance competitiveness".

- "America's Best Plant Award" from _Industry Week_

Magazine for "the company's ISO 9001 successful registration, concurrent engineering technology, cycle time reductions for manufacturing and new product designs, streamlining the organization, cost reduction and environmental leadership".

- "Virginia Quality Factory of the Year Award" from Virginia Senators Robb and Warner

I point these results out to highlight how business performance can be accelerated at a very high rate and achieve high levels of success.

A good business leader must be able to cause and deliver success during good and challenging times. Establishing a culture of rapid change is paramount. Insisting on a never-ending desire for performance improvement is a must. Unleashing the talents of a higher percentage of employees, guided by a prescribed methodology for instituting change, is the prescription for how good leaders achieve exceptional results.

Use the VPM process to change the way you run your business. Put the time into it. Get your 70% hitting on all cylinders. Bring your business through these rapidly changing times as a high performance, and team based, organization. Enjoy the situation and results!

Takeaways are as follows:

I. Insist on numerical definitions of success.

II. Establish an implementation and reporting system and share progress and results widely. What's your BLRC look like?

III. Communicate results in the open, use high employee traffic areas to show progress.

IV. Employ symbols, what would your high-speed clock be?

V. Seek outside recognition of your achievements to validate your programs and achievements. Consider writing articles on business subjects pertinent to the business you are in and have them published. Join associations active in the industry your business serves. Make public significant events, new products, new business attained, in other words one of the duties of a Leader is to create a high profile for your business.

VI. Set stretch goals for those doing the implementation work.

VII. Recognize success, reward those involved and learn from mistakes.

CHAPTER 6:

Leadership

The Vision Powered Management process assumes that a business has in place a leader that possesses certain skills. I identify in this chapter what are the most important skills and characteristics necessary for the successful implementation of the VPM process.

The chapter also provides an exam-like method for identifying leadership strengths and weaknesses in existing and aspiring leaders. Many of the skills are learnable so both current skills and weakness areas can be improved through additional learning.

These skills are presented in four separate categories: individual skills, external or interpersonal skills, creative skills and finally hands-on skills. The chapter is concluded with a listing of actions and traits that leaders must do to optimize their effectiveness in achieving high levels of business performance in these demanding times.

INDIVIDUAL SKILLS

- CONFIDENCE: Do you have high self-confidence? Do you get through the challenges that constantly confront a business and enjoy doing so?

- SYNTHESIS: Are you able to quickly sift through and consolidate details? Can you rapidly conclude what needs to happen, prioritize action and delegate responsibility quickly?

- VISION: Can you easily see where things need to be improved? Can you quickly grasp the big picture and explain it to others? Can you create with others a compelling vision of the future, and have them embrace that vision? Do you like to aim for great things?

- INITIATIVE: Do you act quickly to solve problems? Do you admit and learn from your mistakes? Are you naturally energetic?

- CONTROL: Do you enjoy being in charge? Do you like making decisions? Are you good at convincing others to support your decisions?

- RISK TOLERANCE: Are you comfortable taking risks? Can you make decisions when the facts are uncertain? Do you assess the level of risk involved in decision making?

- RESILIENCE: Can you quickly pick yourself up when things do not go as planned? Do you learn from your mistakes and failures? Do you stick by your guns when others challenge or disagree with your recommendations and decisions?

EXTERNAL SKILLS

- LEADERSHIP: Can you lead and motivate others to follow you and deliver on your decisions? Do others have confidence in your decision making? Are you an effective communicator? Are you good at selecting high performing people?

- COMMUNICATION: Are you competent with many types of communication? Verbal, email, tweets, video? Are you proud, comfortable and confident of your communication skills? Do people easily understand your directions?

- LISTENING: Do you hear what others are telling you? Do you easily understand others when they are communicating to you? Are you a patient listener?

- PERSONAL RELATIONS: Are you emotionally intelligent? Emotional Intelligence is your ability to get smarter with your emotions. It means your emotions don't pull you into bad decisions, and it allows you to be a more effective leader. Self-awareness as well as socially adept leaders who can empathize with others make the most effective leaders.

- NEGOTIATION: Can you stake out a position and defend it when necessary? Can you resolve differences of opinion in a positive way? Do you take the time to carefully prepare yourself for a negotiation?

- ETHICS: Do you deal with others based on respect, fairness and truthfulness? Do you ever bend the rules to get your way? Do you insist others behave ethically?

- SELF DRIVEN: Do you self-start, or do you need someone to pull your starter rope?

CREATIVE THINKING SKILLS

- PROBLEM SOLVING: Do you have the knack for thinking of solutions for problems? Can you quickly identify what the problem is when confronted with a problem? Do you think out of the box easily? Do you recognize opportunities when they present themselves?

- NEW IDEAS: Have you ever had a patent issued? Do you like thinking about edgy and very new ideas for products?

HANDS-ON SKILLS

- GOAL SETTING: Do you use and depend on data to set goals? Do you believe in establishing challenging goals, creating plans to achieve them, can you carry out those plans or delegate that to others?

- PLANNING: Do you require people to develop and schedule tasks for implementing programs and action plans to achieve goals efficiently and effectively?

- DECISION MAKING: Do you make decisions based on relevant information and by weighing the potential outcomes? Are you generally confident in your decision making?

- BUSINESS KNOWLEDGE: Do you strive to have a good general knowledge of the main functional areas of business i.e. sales, marketing, finance, time management, products, and operations?

- ENTREPRENEURIAL KNOWLEDGE: Do you understand how entrepreneurs raise capital? Have you ever turned around a struggling business into a successful one? Do you like taking risk with your own money? Do you like to gamble?

It is a worthwhile exercise for individuals to answer each of the questions posed above. Assign a grading scale from 1 to 5 for each question where 1 represents little or no skill and 5 a high level of skill. There are 54 questions with a maximum score of 270. Assume a person scores less than 165 and then identify by category each question where your response was 3 or less. Then rank each of the categories by the number of questions which have scores of 3 or less.

For example, let's say you had the highest number of 3 or less scores in External Skills followed by Hands-on Skills. Then identify where the 3's or less occurred, creating a list of where you have weaknesses. By doing so you are identifying areas needing improvement that may or may not be learnable. Look to your strengths. Are there strengths you can use to leverage your weaknesses? For the skills that are learnable, pursue ways to strengthen those areas through reading, classwork, etc., so you become a more effective leader. In some cases, you might discover that you would be better off not pursuing a leadership position.

Individuals can wind up in leadership roles for a variety of reasons. They might climb the leadership ladder in various ways, in industries, in civic roles, in education, sports, military fields, politics, etc., or they might start up a new business and oversee its success. The individuals all have some commonality in their skills and the way they conduct themselves in their respective positions. I have listed things that leaders do that contribute to their success based on my experiences of being a leader of businesses for 36 years.

15 ITEMS THAT LEADERS MUST DO

1. THEY CREATE A VISION THAT CRISPLY SUMMARIZES THE PURPOSE OF WHAT THEY ARE OVERSEEING.

2. THEY SET THE PERFORMANCE BAR HIGH BY SETTING DEMANDING GOALS TO ACHIEVE.

3. THEY EXHIBIT HIGH ENERGY, ARE HIGHLY VISIBLE AND COMMUNICATE REGULARLY VIA PRESCRIBED METHODS TO CUSTOMERS, EMPLOYEES, ANALYSTS AND THE INDUSTRY THEY ARE SERVING.

4. THEY ARE PASSIONATE, DECISIVE, FAIR AND INTOLERANT OF EXCUSES.

5. THEY ENCOURAGE BETTER IDEAS, ENJOY CHALLENGES AND FOCUS ON ACTIONS INSTEAD OF WORDS.

6. THEY SURROUND THEMSELVES WITH THE BEST AND THE BRIGHTEST, ENERGETIC AND COMMITTED PEOPLE.

7. THEY DISLIKE BUREAUCRACY AND EMBRACE AMBITIOUS UNDERTAKINGS.

8. THEY ARE QUICK TO CORRECT PERSONNEL ASSIGNMENTS, PROMOTION AND HIRING MISTAKES WHEN CONDITIONS WARRANT CHANGE.

9. THEY CELEBRATE AND REWARD SUCCESS, OPENLY RUFFLE FEATHERS AND ARE WILLING TO LEARN FROM FAILURES.

10. THEY ARE NOT AFRAID TO BREAK FROM THE PACK WHEN NEEDED TO MAKE THINGS HAPPEN.

11. THEY MAKE PROFIT AND FREE CASH FLOW PART OF

THE BUSINESS DNA AND ARE INTOLERANT OF TIME AND MONEY MISSES.

12. THEY PREFER LEAN, FLAT AND FAST-MOVING ORGA-NIZATIONS THAT EMPHASIZE "BRAIN VS. BRAWN".

13. THEY BELIEVE IN AND PROVIDE TRAINING AND EDU-CATION PROGRAMS FOR EMPLOYEES.

14. THEY ENCOURAGE GOOD HEALTH, EXERCISE AND NO SMOKING PROGRAMS FOR ALL EMPLOYEES.

15. THEY DEMAND ETHICAL BEHAVIOR BY ALL, COMPLI-ANCE WITH LAWS, RULES AND REGULATIONS, MU-TUAL RESPECT AND POLITENESS BY ALL.

I will close this chapter with quotations that I always kept in mind during my years in business.

1. "Great men are ordinary men with extra ordinary determination," Abraham Lincoln, U.S. President.

2. "Your words have the power to start or quench passion," Tom Watson, Founder of IBM.

3. "Good leadership consists of showing average people how to do the work of superior people," John D. Rockefeller, American Oil Industry Business Magnate.

4. "Skills make you rich, not theories," Steve Jobs, Founder of Apple.

5. "When you give a directive, make sure people act quickly," Bob Collins, Author/VP GE.

6. "When you join my organization, if you aren't fired up with enthusiasm, you'll be fired with enthusiasm," Vince Lombardi, NFL Football Coach.

7. "A good leader takes more than his share of the blame, and less share of the credit," Arthur Glashow.

8. "If your actions inspire others to dream more, learn more, do more and become more, you are a leader," John Quincy Adams.

CHAPTER 7.

How Emotional Quotient [EQ] can boost nearly every leadership skill

As I look upon the road map with specific action steps that Bob Collins has laid out, I am heartened that we have fulfilled our mission for providing a practical playbook for leaders to lead with vision. Within the voluminous yet explicit content of Bob's recommendations, examples and action steps, there is a point by point road map for the reader to follow.

In Chapter 6 we see his categorical self-assessment for determining your capacity to lead with vision. He specifically directs us to ask ourselves, "Are you emotionally intelligent?" It's a big question and we would be leaving our students short if we didn't give you at least a bit of insight into not only how one might come to know their level of EQ, but how to develop it in earnest.

Nearly every one of Bob's recommended skills for leaders have their roots in EQ. Yet it is often dismissed as the "touchy feely" side of human behavior and thus for the soft at heart, or even to some megalo-maniacs way of thinking "soft in the head". Yet they are entirely wrong-headed in that assessment as the facts don't support their theory. The promise of EQ development in strengthening the expansion of a leader's skills is well documented from over 20 years of empirical research. Even Jack Welch, Bob Collins' colleague and boss at GE acknowledged the importance of these skills when he said, "No doubt, emotional intelligence is rarer than book-smarts, but my experience says it is actually more important in the making of a leader."

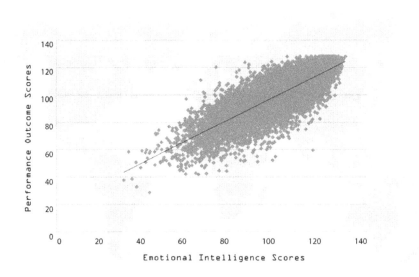

The graphic above summarizes some of the research from over 100,000 people world- wide in the link between EQ and superior performance. The performance outcomes along the left side of the graph are measured in categories that you will see in the Fed Ex example. For instance; influence, decision making, quality of life and health are among the essential keys to be an effective leader. As the graph above points out, with rising EQ scores, the outcomes correspond in kind.

Simply put; humans drive performance in your organizations, and humans are driven by emotions. No man or woman has ever successfully led, either in their organizations or their lives who had limited abilities in the personal mastery category. You may be asking, what defines success in the performance studies cited above? Here's the results of EQ training measured in those areas by the shipping giant Fed Ex.

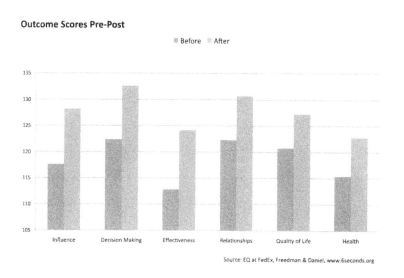

Outcome Scores Pre-Post

Source: EQ at FedEx, Freedman & Daniel, www.6seconds.org

You can see that they are holistic in nature but are closely related to some of Bob Collins' 15 THINGS A LEADER MUST DO, listed in Chapter 6. The compelling part of EQ is that every area cited above is measurable, pre and post implementation, and the results are of course measurable per the VPM method as well.

Let's look at the competencies (there are between 6 and 8 depending on whose school you adhere to) for Emotional Intelligence, as well as some simple steps to begin building your personal mastery.

I am a practitioner and coach for the Six Seconds methodology which gives students workable, practical approaches to expanding their emotional intelligence across the 8 competencies. The 8 are categorized into three actionable steps which we refer to as Know, Choose and Give. I will explain how that helps you get stronger in a moment. Let's look at them here:

Know, Choose, Give Steps

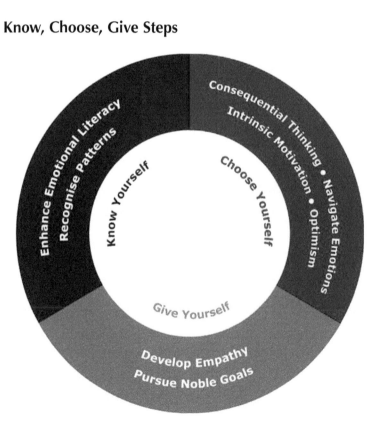

Humans have a capacity to grow within all 8 competencies. That's the good news. The challenging part I find in coaching and teaching is getting established leaders to get started on the basics. It's like a child that wants to play guitar like Jimi Hendrix or Stevie Ray Vaughn but doesn't want to learn their scales.

When we work with teams within organizations, we put the leadership teams through the SEI® Leadership assessment. The SEI® gives us insight into the leaders' levels across all 8 competencies as well as the success factors highlighted in the outcomes graphic above. There are other credible EQ assessments out there. My experience is rooted in this model and it works for me. Let's look at the 8 competencies in more detail.

Enhancing emotional literacy - In study after study the ability to harness the energy of our emotions and thus have more mastery over ourselves as well as "catch" ourselves when we start down an emotionally charged path starts with engaging our cognitive part of our brains. In practicing emotional literacy, we become more aware of the nuanced threads of emotions that run in our bodies. Emotions are valuable. They trigger biochemical storms within us. These storms become an ally to us when we get better at identifying what they are at any given time. Accurately "reading" the emotional data is essential for being intelligent with feelings, both understanding and being able to manage them.

There are extremes to emotional literacy. At the unaware end, a leader can get overwhelmed by them and it can make them irrational. They can also respond in barking as Bob pointed out earlier. Changing from 'barking" to formulating questions and coaching is a level of personal mastery that comes to us through emotional intelligence. When stressed, leaders can default to ruling by numbers as they historically treat their emotions as a sign of weakness. At the other end, a strong emotional vocabulary enables a sense of insight and mastery. Such leaders can express emotional ideas or connect on an intuitive basis more easily.

Recognizing patterns - By acknowledging your emotions as they hit you, we become better prepared to understand what we "do" with them. By acknowledging frequently recurring reactions and behaviors, we can better set ourselves up to respond with more intentionality. All humans have "hot-buttons" that get pressed from time to time. If left to our "instinct" we follow patterns that bring about misunderstanding, discord and fear. Recognizing our patterns more effectively can set us up for real self -mastery.

Consequential thinking - Applying consequential thinking means that we are more intentional in evaluating the costs and benefits of our choices. It is a key in managing our impulses and being less reactive. As leaders are looked to in every organization to provide strategic planning for their teams, a leader with high levels of consequential thinking is best positioned to put the team on track and moving toward its mission.

Navigate Emotions - One of the misconceptions of involving emotions in driving human behavior is that if we are in an "emotional place" we will make a bad decision. While the "emotional decision being a poor one" can sometimes be true, from an emotional intelligence standpoint, having the ability to harness the emotions is a higher form of self-mastery. The emotions have the power to energize us toward accomplishing what we want.

Understanding they are a source of valuable insight; competent leaders can transform them to feelings that are helpful to themselves and to others.

Intrinsic Motivation - The definition of intrinsic motivation might be to say it is how we gain energy from personal values and commitments versus being driven by external forces. Extrinsically motivated individuals by contrast depend on what others say or behave toward them and rely on a reward system to gain their sense of worth. Extrinsically motivated people are on a track to reduce their self-efficacy. Intrinsically Motivated leaders are more able to stand up, challenge the status quo, take risks, and persevere when the skies remain stormy for a long time.

Optimism - By taking a proactive perspective of hope and possibility, we are exercising optimism. Everyone will draw from both pools of optimistic and pessimistic points of view every day of the week. On one end of the spectrum, we can blame others, use victim thinking and see ourselves as powerless. Sometimes this is thought of by the person afflicted with a pessimistic view of being "practical" or pragmatic and over analyzing risks. The other end of the spectrum we take responsibility for finding our solutions and persevere through obstacles.

Develop Empathy - Our capacity to recognize and respond appropriately to others' emotions is a good place to start the competency of developing empathy. It's a nonjudgmental openness to what others are feeling as well as their experiences. By validating and responding in a way that shows you are concerned, you build trust that supports your ability to lead.

Pursue Noble Goal - Leaders that consistently connect their daily choices to their overarching sense of purpose create a foundation for leadership which is not easily shaken. This competency activates all the other competencies in the list. A noble goal is something that we connect our meaning to in our work role as well as our time spent away from work. At one extreme a leader with low levels of this competency lives for the short term and is constantly putting out fires. They may be easily swayed by others and exhibit tendencies such as short-term avoidance or avoiding discomfort. A strong dose of this results in making better decisions and transforming feelings on a deep level.

One of the best methods to start on your journey to developing your EQ is to start with the basics. It seems frustratingly simple, but the emotional storms hit us every day. Whether it's dealing with frustration, or anger, or jealousy which can lead us to a negative pattern when somebody pushes our buttons.

The first step then is to know yourself. We do this by coaching our executives to begin writing down in a journal (so you can work toward a goal) for how many times you cognitively thought about the feelings you were experiencing in any given moment. This makes many Alpha types uncomfortable for they are impatient. Give it time. When Bob Collins talks about converting cops to coaches, this is the hard work done with every personality type. EQ builds these self-awareness muscles and sets up leaders for success.

A second action point is to know what your patterns are. When someone acts in a particular way or behaves in a meeting a certain way, does this trigger a pattern for how you move forward? In my business career I learned that I had a rebellious nature to me. When someone would want me to do a certain thing a certain way, I would grind my teeth and figure out a way to do it my own way. Autonomy is tremendously important to me and my values. I also tended to respond (and not in a positive way) to someone exerting control over my time or process.

Once I became aware of my pattern, I was able to write a new script for myself. For instance, when I felt myself getting angry or frustrated about something in my personal life, I would recognize that my pattern would be to stew about it. I began utilizing the competency of navigating emotions to get to a more productive place. In this case I would write a script in my brain when I felt a particular way, and I would get curious about the persons motivation rather than fly off the handle and stew about their actions.

Pretty simple when you read it here on the page, very difficult to do in the moment. That's why the limbic part of the brain requires motivation, and reflection, for it to learn these new skills.

CHAPTER 8:

Looking to the Future

With the concentration of businesses via mergers and acquisitions, coupled with the drive toward eliminating non-value-added internal business functions, business has been through a sea change in the last 20 years.

For example, in a walkthrough of a typical company, one would see that where a separate system used to exist for orders received, personnel data, financial records, etc., they have switched to one overall system providing all its data needs. Segments of product manufacturing have been outsourced to a lower cost company. In-house data storage systems are now on Cloud computing and storage. The decentralization of internal computing sources moved to the points where the work is done. The proliferation of high speed, high capacity data networking brings this all together to create a new and very different business world.

In addition, the introduction and use of artificial intelligence, robotics, embedded product computers, pattern recognition technologies, and digital footprints are creating systems that are capable of self-sensing, self-controlling, and self-optimizing. In fact, some systems are now predicting what will likely happen in the immediate future! As products, engineering and manufacturing processes become more digital, the total business equation becomes more variable and changes dramatically. New channels for growing a business emerge, both decentralization and localization of manufacturing of products become logical, the need for optimization of supply chains rises in level of importance both for cost and time reasons, and the need to deploy more and more intelligence into the business systems accelerates. For example, the rise of technologies such as digital additive manufacturing creates the opportunity for brand new design and manufacturing processes.

As the physical aspects of the design and manufacturing become more and more entwined with digital technology it leads to less reliance on human hands-on involvement and intervention in the traditional business processes. For example, workers now close to existing production process, i.e. the "making process", will have to learn new skills in areas such as mechanical and electronic troubleshooting, machine programming and quality optimization. Rerouting of business employees into "watch dog" or "air traffic" or "systems control-like" positions is already underway.

These changes taken together will continue to create significant new and very different business and personnel opportunities. With the rise of more global opportunities, the criticality of the management and protection of intellectual property, and the collaboration with new business partnership becomes more and more necessary. These changes will require business leaders to continue to move toward a new and very different corporate culture. Leaders of the future will have less to do with managerial hierarchy, and command and control decision making. They will have to be able to combine their internal operational excellence of the past with a new skill set that will enable them to focus on technological development and new market and product opportunities. Business collaborations will become more and more of a requirement.

Leaders are going to have to move away from going it alone and recognize that the command and control philosophy coupled with a few partnering strategies will simply not work in this complicated, hi-speed, interwoven digital economy of the future. Leaders will have to spend more time on business strategies, horizontal business expansions, global collaborative activities, personnel hiring, training and retention strategies, and product expansions. They will need to foster a culture where employees become sentries for product improvements and expansions. As you all know Amazon has disrupted businesses from Bookstores to Supermarkets. Amazon is a business that leverages technology for the disruption of conventional business methods. As a result, its employees must also be capable of adapting to these rapid deployments of technology throughout the business. Amazon rolled out a plan in 2019 to retrain one third of its US workforce over a six-year period, about 100,000 employees, at a cost of $700 million. This isn't charity because Amazon is acting in its self-interest to retain workers so that they can keep up with their technology advances. It's an illustration on a large scale of what future business leaders will have to contend with as a result of not enough workers being available that possess these high-tech skills

As job complexities and skill levels increase due to the adoption of the technologies mentioned above, so will coaching have to rely on more sophisticated methods to deal with these changes. We are already seeing the use of "coaching apps" being adopted into the workplace.

For example, a new artificial intelligence [A-I] coach training app named 'Coach Amanda', powered by IBM's Watson® Supercomputer, is now available. It is a chat-bot that makes suggestions regarding time management and performance reviews. Other coaching apps, such as Humu®, are directed at improving corporate culture.

Just as the extensible nature and performance of the Internet allows it to scale so dramatically, businesses will need to operate in a similar manner. Ongoing training, reshuffling and redirecting of employees into differing tasks and positions, while still leveraging the minds, creativity and commitment of employees, becomes more and more important in this new business world.

As readers of this chapter know, some surgeries today are performed by the surgeon sitting in a control room manipulating robotic surgery on a patient. I can envision employees sitting in NASA like control rooms managing all the business processes, utilizing computer business software systems, and machines, as they implement customer orders through delivery.

Despite all this change, I remain encouraged by what I see happening in many of today's businesses. The Manufacturing Leadership Council [MLC], part of the National Association of Manufacturers [NAM], highlights new activities being employed in businesses and progress being made. To illustrate this, I've included some quotes from recent articles:

"Our cultural glue is giving employees the power to make decisions and also for them to be accountable for their outcomes."

"Keys to our success are integrated business teams that function on a foundation of collaboration and trust."

"Employees are cross-trained on a variety of production functions and equipment to allow for flexibility in job assignments."

"Performance monitoring and continuous communication between levels of the organization builds a companywide accountability mindset."

"One of our biggest challenges is the sheer volume of data that we now enjoy. The question is what do we do with all this digital exhaust? In the end we must be able to sort through and determine what data has no value, toss it and then find ways to leverage the data that does have value."

"Leadership of the future will need more and more to rely on aptitude and attitude if we are going to be successful in fulfilling our vision of improving Customer value."

Larry Culp, the new CEO of General Electric, my

alma mater, stated in the GE 2019 Annual report the following:

"We need to shift our lens back to the customer and work backwards to improve what matters to them. If we do this successfully, our own growth and performance will follow. We can't win unless our customers win."

He went on to say, "We need to focus our attention on the things that matter the most, so we can move them the furthest." "This kind of work takes time. But it's work we can no doubt do." "We have to prioritize our cash generation in each of our businesses." "We have eliminated Headquarters layers to improve accountability." "First and most important is our team. One of the first things I did as CEO was to meet and talk with GE people." "Our Aviation team used lean and digital tools to improve average cycle time to produce one of our newest jet engines, the LEAP engine, by 10 days, a 36 % reduction. This led to lower inventory levels, more efficient throughput and more available cash. We are also removing waste and increasing speed across our supply chains-from our suppliers, through our factories and into our customers' workflows."

Larry Culp was hired by the GE Board of Directors to overcome almost two decades of management misdeeds that brought the company from one of the best, to one of the worst. In thinking about these few sentences highlighting Culp's views on what needs to change in GE, as well as the MLC highlighted quotes above, I ask the readers to note the key phrases that echo a lot of what the Vision Powered Management process entails.

Please take your time to do this. Despite the similarities with what the VPM process prescribes, the basic difference and value of the VPM process is that it provides a "how-to tool kit" structure for leaders to utilize in dealing with their businesses. The business could be a startup, one that is expanding, or a mature business.

It is a tool kit that can stand the test of time since I was employing many of these tools successfully starting in the late 80's. At the heart of the process is:

1. Gaining the support of a large majority of the business employees participating in and believing in the process.

2. And, using a structured process to guide what to do and a method to track and communicate progress being made.

I encourage current and aspiring leaders to utilize the ideas and principles of Vision Powered management. Next generation leaders must be able to develop and/or modify an organization that thirsts to evaluate new technologies quickly, that can recognize the need for and adopt new business models quickly, hatch new business systems, products and partnerships when required and avoid tempting but not viable opportunities. You will be participating in a very exciting period of both change and opportunity.

Formula for Success . . .

- Not another program – won't happen overnight
- A vision that is articulated and understood
- Time devoted by business leader – genuine involvement / commitment is key
- Some business leaders need coaching / counseling more than others – learning new behaviors
- Requires significant resources – time, money, people
- "Nothing Sacred" targets / take risks and "Let Go"
- Business leaders' fast and decisive action on recommendations
- Commitment to training is critical
- Get maximum involvement
- Celebrate successes and champions – communicate and reinforce at every opportunity

Our readers are also encouraged to next visit Chapter 9, a case study of a growing mid-size company. The XYZ company is struggling with how best to deal with its plans to not only accelerate its rate of growth, but also to improve the profitability and cash flow of the business simultaneously. The case study provides an opportunity for the reader to apply many of the principles of Vision Powered Management and to apply the process to either their current or planned businesses.

I will close this chapter of the book with quotations that support the concepts contained in the Vision Powered Management process.

"What is success? I think it is a mixture of having the flair for the thing that you are doing, knowing that it is not enough, that you have got to have hard work and a certain kind of purpose," Margaret Thatcher, Prime Minister of England.

"An automobile goes nowhere efficiently unless it has a hot spark to ignite things, to set the cogs of the machine in motion. So, I try to make every player on my team feel like they are the spark that keeps our machine in motion. On them depends our success," Knute Rockne, Head Coach of Football, Notre Dame University.

"Every man of action has a strong dose of egotism, pride, hardness and cunning. But all those things will be regarded as high qualities only if he can make them the means to achieve great ends," Charles De Gaulle, President of the Fifth Republic of France.

My favorite is the ancient Chinese poem that states, "Go to the people. Learn from them. Love them. Start with what they know. Build on what they have. But of the best leaders, when their task is accomplished, and their work is done, the people will remark, WE HAVE DONE IT OURSELVES."

Remember that true empowerment is possible only when the leader and the employees learn to live and thrive in the paradox of empowerment and contradiction.

CHAPTER 9:

A VPM Practice Case Study

The value of a book such as this becomes a reality only if the reader can apply much of what has been read into practice. As Authors, our ideal objective is that we have been successful in introducing our readers to ideas about business management and leadership that they will want to apply in their current and future careers. As a result, this chapter is intended to allow a reader to engage in a real-life situation in which a growing company wanted to embark on the next step of more effectively dealing with current growth. At the same time also positioning the company for more aggressive global growth.

At the end of this Case Study we suggest that the reader take on the position of the CEO and apply steps of the VPM process that they would employ in implementing the change process. We provide some assistance to the reader by suggesting that they address and develop their own answers to the 10 questions at the end of the Study.

The XYZ company is a mid-size industrial business located

in upstate New York. The annual sales in 2017 are $200 Million, and the company has been growing for the past years at 8% per year. See the XYZ Company Financial Statement in the Appendix for further details. Currently the XYZ Company is divided into two physical locations. The first location is dedicated to the development, production, and sales of a product line that is focused on industrial electronic safety equipment. [Hereafter referred to as ESE that stands for Electronic Safety Equipment]. The second location produces develops custom-machining centers containing modern Computer Numerical Control [CNC] electronics and motors as well as producing custom machined high precision parts for its customer base. The CNC electronics and motors run the machining centers automatically. [This product organization is hereafter referred to as MCM that stands for Modern CNC Machines]. MCM also supports ESE's machining needs for their product line, as well as selling machining custom work for its own customer base. The Parent XYZ company is currently undergoing a location move to consolidate both locations into one physical complex and streamline the organization functions of each division. In addition, it is seeking ways to benefit from the combined workforce that would enable faster global growth.

Each of the two organizations has its own rules, roles, goals, policies, technology, etc. Currently both ESE and MCM maintain their own respective policies and procedures. Each facility has a manager who oversees their rules, roles, technology, environments, goals and policies. With respect to customer interactions MCM has a customer base focused in the United States [U.S.]; as such, MCM's policies and rules regarding contracts, shipping, etc., are more uniform as they are dictated by U.S. national trade law and state trade laws. However, ESE maintains a global customer base; therefore, many of its customer-related rules and policies are more varied and fluid in order to adapt to the changing needs associated with globalization. The simplicity of MCM's customer interactions, as well as the custom nature of the work performed at this facility, allows MCM to operate a very simple marketing and sales department. Many of the sales policies are dictated by the Marketing and Sales assessment of the needs and requirements of each customer's job request.

In some cases, the sales contract is directly negotiated by the individual sales engineer and customer without involvement from the company's upper management. Due to the complexities of globalization, this type of simplicity is not possible for the sales department at ESE. Therefore, ESE has rules and policies in place stating that international orders must be reviewed by management in order to determine whether outside legal consultation is necessary. This ensures compliance with each importing country's trade regulations towards incoming products from the U.S. as well as the regulations of the US regarding exportation to these countries.

The pending merger of ESE and MCM sales and marketing organizations requires an analysis of the respective differences for customer interactions and reconciliation into a common system. The CEO of the parent company has decided that merging the sales groups from both entities into one department is economically and logistically the most effective result. It will require that a new face of the combined business be developed for the combined customer base and employees will need revised rules and guidelines for the new organization. From a structural standpoint, this merger also requires that the combined marketing and sales forces personnel be trained and educated in new policies or rules allowing them to service both customer bases' needs. Each person needs to learn about both business's products, customers and competitors. In other words, the creation of a new functional structural framework.

In this instance, MCM had a sales structure that was more autonomous of upper management. In addition, the domestic nature of MCM's sales created an environment in which many of the details of each customer transaction could easily be assumed or identified through simple means [shipping provider resources, U.S. or state government websites, etc.]. This is in stark contrast to ESE's sales department's structure, which relies heavily on sales personnel interacting with upper management and possibly outside legal resources for knowledge needed to conduct global transactions. Tension will exist while determining how best to implement this combination.

In this instance, the company sales are increasing in both facilities and the company is growing at a solid rate. MCM's high precision machining centers are getting exposure to the Canadian automotive market and requests for quotations are increasing as a result. ESE's market focus has primarily been on industrial furnaces. Recently some offshore drilling platform companies have expressed interest in their technology for emergency shutdown of undersea oil drilling equipment. The decision to merge the marketing and sales force allows better utilization of existing resources to meet these growing needs. The strategy assumes that in doing so, new hiring will not be necessary initially, thus minimizing the potential to shed staff if the company experiences an economic downturn. Furthermore, the learning of new skills required by each sales staff member in order to understand and complete sales demands for both MCM and ESE products carries with it an increase in training expenses. Staff member's knowledge levels must expand so that they understand and become expert in a broader range of products and the complexities of dealing with both US and global customers. This creates an opportunity for salary growth commensurate with increased responsibility and higher skill levels. Management is hoping that by investing in the existing personnel, staff retention will remain consistent [management is satisfied with the quality of the current staff], allowing for future profitable growth savings resulting in job protection.

This case study presents the readers an opportunity to engage in many of the steps of the VPM process. Examples of tasks to be considered are as follows:

1. Could you develop a Vision Statement for the combined company that the employees would rally behind? Develop at least two Vision statements for the combined business, keeping each statement to no more than two sentences. For example: "Leverage our proven, reliable computer and software technology to enable rapid profitable growth in new markets".

2. Would you want to have a different overall business goal than profitability? If so, what would that be that would result in the employees rallying around the changes? For example: "Invest smartly in our technology to support new global market growth profitably".

3. Would there be value in creating a new business name that would inspire excitement about the change? List at least

two names, each of which ties into the Vision Statements you create above. For example, the company could be named "Precision Automatic Systems" since both product lines utilize computer technology to create products that control equipment automatically. This also encourages the organization to look broadly for new markets needing such equipment.

4. Can you develop a scenario on how you would leverage the concepts of teamwork and empowerment to convince the two independent marketing and sales teams that one combined team is better than two independent teams? List the benefits such as cross training that would accrue to them. Examples might be more, and higher skill levels allow growth into higher paying jobs.

5. What opportunities do you see to "sell" the combined organization to the entire group of employees in the Company? In other words, what would the combination do for all employees? Make a list of those benefits. For example, one benefit would be that by employee learning and using new and more complex skills, future salary growth becomes available.

6. What elements of EQ might apply here that would be helpful in making the transition smooth and eliminate any resistance to change? Elements such as Optimism, Develop Empathy and Pursue a Common Goal. List those benefits.

7. What other business goals besides growth would you highlight that you would want to achieve as a result of this combination? Are there any items needing improvement

that you can identify from the XYZ Company Financial statement? What additional information would you request to allow you to dig deeper into product sales of each organization? List them and describe what action steps you would recommend. As an example, request financial data on sales of products by model number in each product group, i.e. ESE and MCM. Find out if after market pricing can be increased as a means of improving profitability. Is the company investing more into products whose sales are growing more rapidly than others? Request a financial statement for each ESE and MCM product lines to determine their individual levels of profitability and growth.

8. Do you see an opportunity to apply any of the steps of "Clearing the Decks" to this situation that would generate improved business performance? If so, make your own list of those steps. For example: Does the combination of the product lines allow for the elimination of certain procedures that may be redundant that would free up time of personnel to work on more fruitful activities? Should the sales and marketing combination activity be expanded? See question 11.

9. Can you envision creating a team of employees to work on prioritizing activities to improve on matters that serve to support a new Vision statement? For example: to identify new markets that are opportunity rich to market the existing technology? For example: MSM's CNC products for control of robots and plastic molding machines instead of just metal cutting machinery. Task the team to prioritize and develop a step by step implementation plan of action

to implement their recommendations. Have them develop their Structured Framework for implementation along the lines of the VPM structured framework in Chapter 4.

10. What characteristics of Leadership do you believe would be most helpful in reaching a successful combination of the two organization's? List those and compare your own skill set to that listing.

11. What other organization combination possibilities do you see that might add further value to this process? For example: to include a common design organization, or manufacturing organization, or employee relations organization. List what those other changes would be and what benefit you would expect to result

12. Do you believe you have adequate leadership skills that would enable you to lead this type of organization change? Were your personal scores from the Leadership evaluation test suggested in VPM Chapter 6 high enough to give you confidence that you fit the definition of a leader? Are you ready to strengthen any of your skills that might need improvement? If so, list what action you might take to overcome any weak areas.

The point of going through the case study is to illustrate to our readers its applicability to most every kind of business situation. It requires the leader to examine the performance of an existing business, or to think through the strategy for a new business, or to prioritize the most important activities to undertake, either in developing a new business, expanding an existing good business or fixing or improving the performance of an existing business. It also forces a self-evaluation of your current leadership skills. It can surface areas that can be strengthened through education. It also may identify that your aspiration should not be as a leader but perhaps be the inventor of a new business or the person responsible for strategic changes in the direction of a business. Then one can concentrate on finding an outstanding leader for your team while you focus on technology or marketing, or fund raising.

As Authors we would recommend highly that the reader go through and answer the above questions in a written fashion since the act of writing reinforces the lessons learned.

Let us close by saying how excited we are that this book came together. We sincerely hope that the pragmatic approach helps you in having a clearer understanding of what to do as a visionary leader. Vision Powered Management [VPM] takes you there, and places you in the best position to succeed. Please keep in contact with the authors to let us know how your VPM journey is treating you! It is our sincere hope that this Vision Powered Management book will have a lasting impact on your careers as business leaders in the 21st century.

Acknowledgements

Wall Street Journal reporting on new technologies impacting on Manufacturing 2019

National Association of Manufacturers articles on What's New in Manufacturing 2019

Manufacturing Leadership Council interviews 2019

Various articles regarding the Polaris Missile system

Various articles on Leadership characteristics

GE Workout Process

GE Annual Report, Larry Culp, Chairman and CEO, 2018 Letter to Shareowners

Financial definitions

President John F. Kennedy, September 12, 1962, "Moon Speech", Rice Stadium, Rice University, Houston Texas.

Heritage Foundation Lectures July 20, 2006, Reagan's Vision

"Culture eats strategy for breakfast"-Peter Drucker

APPENDIX 1.

Vision Powered Management Report Card

Measurements	Target YTD	Actual YTD	Grade YTD	Comments
Orders Received	$75 M	$92 M	A+	Expecting to exceed target total year by 20%
Sales Delivered	$68 M	$78 M	A+	Will exceed total year target
Profit %/Sales	15%	12%	B-	YTD Sales include lower margin products, expect to hit total year target
Free Cash Flow	$10.2 M	$9.36 M	B-	Will meet total year target
Inventory Turns	12 turns	9.6 turns	A-	Estimate 10.5 total year turns
Delivery Promise Kept	100%	96%	B	Estimating 97% total year
BTO Cycle Time	3 weeks	8 weeks	C-	Estimating 6 weeks total year
TTM Cycle Time	18 months	13 months	B+	Estimating 13 months
Quality Cost %/Sales	0.8%	1.1%	B	Estimating 1.0% total year

COMMENTARY

Progress to date is showing improvement in all areas, our teams are working hard to hit the targets. Current total year estimates show significant progress compared to last year. Much work remains to be done with inventory reductions to meet that target. The new BTO, TTM are showing solid progress from the starting points of 6 weeks for BTO and 18 months for TTM.

APPENDIX 2.

Business Financial Terms Definitions

*Receivables Turnover: Total operating revenues divided by **average** receivables. Used to measure how effectively a **firm** is managing its **accounts receivable**.*

*Inventory Turnover: A measure of how often the company sells and replaces its **inventory**. It is the ratio of annual cost of **sales** to the latest **inventory**.*

*Return on Investment: Net **book** income as a proportion of **net book value**.*

*Return on Sales: A measurement of operational efficiency equaling **net** pre-tax **profits** divided by **net sales** expressed as a percentage.*

*Current Ratio: Indicator of **short-term debt-paying ability**. Determined by dividing **current assets** by **current liabilities**. The higher the ratio, the more **liquid** the **company**.*

*Debt/Equity Ratio: Indicator of **financial leverage**. Compares* *assets* provided by *creditors* to assets provided by *shareholders*. Determined by dividing *long-term debt* by common *stockholder equity*.

Free Cash Flow: Cash not required for operations or for *reinvestment*. Often defined as *earnings* before *interest* (often obtained from the operating income line on the *income statement*) less *capital_expenditures* less the change in *working capital*

APPENDIX 3.

Photographs

Jack Welch shaking my hand during our Syracuse meeting.

My first meeting with the legendary Reg
Jones, Chairman and CEO GE.

**Bob Collins with Virginia Senators Robb and Warner
looking on as Bob received the Quality Factory of
the Year Award on behalf of the employees.**

My mentor, Bill Anders. I reported to Bill in my
first senior management position at GE. I learned
a lot from him that I applied in my career.

APPENDIX 4.

XYZ Company Financial Statement

XYZ COMPANY FINANCIAL STATEMENT [$M]

CATEGORY	2016	2017	V%
ORDERS RECEIVED	215M	238M	10.7
SALES	185M	200M	8.1
COST OF GOODS SOLD	61M	66M	5.8
% COGS	33	33	0
SALES AND MARKETING COSTS	18M	20M	11.1
OTHER ADMIN COSTS	91M	95M	4.4
GROSS MARGIN	15M	19M	26.6
GROSS MARGIN %	8	10.5	31.2
TAXES AND OTHER COSTS	2.9M	3.6M	24.1
NET INCOME	13.1M	15.4M	17.6
NET INCOME %	7.1	7.8	9.9
FREE CASH FLOW	10M	13M	30

About the Authors

Robert "Bob" P. Collins is an honors graduate of Manhattan College and winner of its Centennial Award for its Most Outstanding Engineering Graduate. He is a retired officer of the General Electric Company, where he spent 38 years, 13 years of it as a vice president.

He worked in GE's aerospace business for his first 23 years, serving in a variety of aircraft electronics businesses. He participated in all commercial and military aircraft development during that period. He was granted a patent in 1985 for liquid crystal displays used in cockpit instrumentation.

For his last 15 years, he was in the industrial systems business of GE where he led the factory automation business, including the joint venture between GE and Fanuc Ltd., a preeminent Japanese business. During his career, he was VP/CEO/chairman of businesses ranging from $600 million in sales to $1.8 billion.

During his time in the industrial systems business, Collins was active in promoting the modernization of factories and the creation of high-involvement workforces as a means of improving productivity and operational efficiencies. He published in excess of 60 articles on those subjects over that period and was considered an expert in the industry.

During his post-GE career, he served as chairman of the board of directors of Scott Technologies (Nasdaq), chairman of the board of directors of Comdial Corporation (Nasdaq), and director of CSE Global Ltd., a Singapore public company.

He served as chairman of the finance committee and member of the investment, endowment, and capital campaign committees while also serving as a trustee on the board of trustees of St. Anne's-Belfield, a private school located in Charlottesville, Virginia.

Collins is currently the founder and owner of Capstone Consulting and Westover Estates Land Development LLC. He and his wife, Andrea, spend time in Marco Island, Florida, Charlottesville, Virginia, and Camden, Maine, and they are the proud parents of four children and nine grandchildren. They are members of the Island Club in Marco Island, the Megunticook Golf Club of Rockport, Maine, and the Camden, Maine, Yacht Club.

Robert Stillman, MATD, is a senior leadership and development trainer for New Horizons Learning Solutions based in Livonia, Michigan, and regularly teaches business professionals through the company's Center for Leadership Development®.

He has over 25 years of sales, marketing, and project management experience in the environmental, insurance, and IT management industries. He credits the wonderful association with The

Eleven Agency in Irvine, California, and now with New Horizons as being turning points in the realization of his passions and abilities. High-profile engagements with Google (Chrome Book rollout in 2012) and Microsoft and his continued development as a go-to resource for customized training interventions with New Horizons' Fortune 500 clientele give him ample opportunities to work his craft.

Throughout his career, he has made a study of successful leaders and how they bring their visions through to fruition. With this background, he regularly helps executives apply their own vision to bring about exciting changes and results. He studies the intersection of emotional intelligence, improvisational theater skills, and adult learning and what each contributes to the world becoming a better place.

He is a certified practitioner and assessor in EQ (emotional quotient) and uses his improvisational theater (2002 graduate of the Second City's Conservatory) and business background to facilitate workshops and coaching to transform lives and workplaces. A father of five amazing children, he holds a BS in chemistry from Northern Illinois University and a master's in training and development from Roosevelt University.